Keep Me in Your Heart a While

KEEP ME IN YOUR HEART A WHILE

THE HAUNTING ZEN OF
DAININ KATAGIRI

Dosho Port

Wisdom Publications
199 Elm Street
Somerville MA 02144 USA
www.wisdompubs.org

Library of Congress Cataloging-in-Publication Data
Port, Dosho.
 Keep me in your heart awhile : the haunting Zen of Dainin Katagiri / Dosho Port.
  p. cm.
 Includes bibliographical references.
 ISBN 0-86171-568-3 (pbk. : alk. paper)
 1. Katagiri, Dainin, 1928–1990. 2. Spiritual life—Sotoshu. 3. Spiritual life—Zen Bud-
dhism. I. Title.
 BQ968.A87695 2009
 294.3'444092--dc22
                              2008041531

12 11 10 09 08
 5 4 3 2 1

Cover design by Phil Pascuzzo. Interior design by Tony Lulek. Set in Bulmer MT Regular 12/16. Permission granted by Coleman Barks for reprint of translation of Rumi poem
on page 88.

Forgive, O Lord, my little jokes on Thee
And I'll forgive Thy great big one on me.

Robert Frost

For Dainin Katagiri Roshi

Table of Contents

Introduction

There's a train leaving nightly
called "When All Is Said and Done"—
Keep me in your heart for a while
Warren Zevon

"AFTER MY DEATH I will come back and haunt over you, checking your practice." Katagiri Roshi said this frequently, teasing me and my fellow students at the Minnesota Zen Center. I trained under his guidance for thirteen years, from 1977–90, but training is really a moment-by-moment activity. Frankly, some moments I took it up wholeheartedly and some moments I squirmed in order to avoid his direction toward realizing the vast sublime beauty of this life. At times it was just too much.

But as more time passes, I begin to see more and more the indelible imprint Dainin Katigiri left on my heart; increasingly I see the truth and power of his Zen, and that "his" Zen and "mine" are not two things. Today, as I write this introduction, I enter the nineteenth year of practice after Roshi's death. Life-and-death go just like that.

Dainin ("Great Patience") Katagiri was an American Zen pioneer like a handful of other Zen priests who left their Japanese homes beginning in the late 1950s and came to the greening Dharma fields of America. Katagiri spent most of the 1960s helping Shunryu Suzuki with the booming, hippie-filled San Francisco Zen Center. After Suzuki died in 1971, Katagiri came to Minnesota looking for the "real Americans" and founded a rather non-booming Zen Center.

At the time my teacher died, I was thirty-three. I had naïvely vowed to hand on the Dharma that Roshi had worked so unrelentingly to transmit—so unrelentingly that he imagined himself coming back as a ghost to continue his work.

During the early years after his death, I traveled around some, looking for other teachers to round out my training. I did find some good teachers: Toni Packer, Thich Nhat Hanh, Tangen Harada, Shodo Harada, and Daido Loori. I am deeply grateful to each of them.

However, no matter how wonderful the teacher, I kept remembering things Katagiri Roshi had said to me and bearing in mind his subtle forms of training. To this day, I am inspired and informed by Katagiri Roshi's example and instruction. For me, Katagiri Roshi's "haunting" still includes, to borrow a phrase from Warren Zevon, keeping him in my heart for a while.

THIS BOOK IS A COLLECTION of some of the things that I saw, heard, and learned from Dainin Katagiri Roshi, and it's an exploration of what those things mean to me now, as I try to live the Zen he left imprinted on my heart—and what I hope they can come to mean to you, the reader.

I was most moved by Katagiri Roshi in simple moments during casual interactions; these moments were often vivid truth-happening places, evocative of the ancient koans in the Zen tradition. Accordingly, the structure of this book is built around a series of such moments: each chapter starts with an encounter with Katagiri and unfolds from there. In most cases, the names of others have been changed in order to protect the innocent.

And yet, this book you hold in your hands is not a hagiography, a wide-eyed adoring account of a sainted teacher, nor is it a gossipy tell-all. I don't intend to inflate Katagiri Roshi—or to deflate him either, for that matter.

One purpose of this book is to share what it was like to train with one of the first-generation American Zen teachers and in so doing I hope to help preserve and revitalize this incredible way. Another purpose is to offer a perspective, informed by one of America's Zen pioneers, on some of the current trends in Dharma practice.

Katagiri Roshi emphasized zazen as wholehearted surrender rather than using zazen as a means to psychological healing or even to become a buddha. He lived the precepts of conduct as the expression of wonderment rather than moralistic regulations. He taught a Zen that offered no sweet cookies rather than a means to build personal or collective fame and fortune. And Roshi emphasized the central role of the teacher-student relationship.

ONE OF THE THINGS I REMEMBER from sometime in the late 1970s is an observation Roshi made after he returned from his once-a-year visit to San Francisco Zen Center. He said that the images of Suzuki Roshi got bigger and bigger each year. "Soon," Katagiri Roshi joked with his arms open, head tilted back and eyes looking at the heavens, "Suzuki Roshi will be huge like God."

I also remember hearing Katagiri Roshi give a Dharma talk in the early 1980s about one of the Buddha's disciples, Vakkali. When Vakkali was deathly ill, the Buddha came to visit him. Vakkali confessed to the Buddha that he had long yearned to see the "Blessed One." Buddha shut him up. "Enough, Vakkali! One who sees the Dharma sees me; one who sees me, sees the Dharma."

The Buddha handled misplaced adoration with this rough Dharma. *Dharma,* of course, is a Sanskrit word that refers, varyingly and all at once, to the big Truth, the teachings about the big Truth, phenomena themselves, and the way to get things done congruently with the first three meanings.

Like any good teacher, the Buddha yearned for his student Vakkali not to mistake the object of teaching (the Buddha's human form, in this case) with the referent—mistaking the pointing finger for the moon. To really see the Buddha, to really see any teacher, is to see and actualize for oneself what the teacher teaches.

Therefore, keeping my teacher in my heart a while is not really about him or me. And yet it depends on us both—and you too.

My task as Katagiri Roshi's disciple has been to study his Zen and become one with it, and to let him and his teachings haunt me—but not necessarily to agree blindly with him, or to parrot his Dharma back to others. To do so would betray both of us. It is my hope that all of us together might do something small to keep the Buddhadharma alive in our hearts.

THERE ARE MANY PEOPLE I would like to acknowledge for their contribution to this book. I am grateful to the members of Clouds in Water Zen Center who generously supported me and my family for a dozen years prior to 2004. I am grateful to my parents, Bob and Jean Port, because among other things they taught me to love. I am grateful to my children, Lily and Gar, because among other things they gave me this life. I am grateful to Tomoe Katagiri, my spiritual mother, for telling me to stand up straight and smile when I needed it most. I am grateful for the kindness of Elizabeth Andrew, Walter Bera, Susan Bourgerie, Nonin Chowaney, Paul Dosho Courtney, John Cowen, Janith Hatch, John Hatch, Ken Port, and many in the Minneapolis Public Schools. I am grateful to the students at Wild Fox Zen, Transforming Through Play Temple, for testing what follows in the past, present, and future. I am grateful for the editing and proofreading of Janith Hatch, Christina Nguyen, and Wisdom's rough Josh Bartok. Finally, I am grateful for Tetsugan for her friendship, love, and steady support. Her careful way of examining these ideas and my writing through many incarnations has helped me clarify and express what I've found to write from this broken hill.

1. Not Getting Zen

Three days before Katagiri Roshi died, he spoke by telephone with Socho Koshin Ogui, a long-time friend and minister in the Pure Land tradition. "You know, Koshin," Katagiri Roshi said, "Zen is very difficult."

Ogui-san replied, "Well, there's nothing to worry about."

PERHAPS WITH DEATH IMMINENT Katagiri Roshi was traveling through a moment of desire for something other than death. One of Roshi's favorite stories, guaranteed to result in him laughing wildly at his own un-joke, was about a famous Zen master who was about to die. When his disciples came to him expecting his last words to reflect the essence of the profound, ultimate meaning of the Ancestors, he quietly said to them, "I don't want to die."

Another view of Roshi's "difficult Zen" is that he was quietly facing death, practicing the difficult Zen of living the life at hand, even when that meant being a body wracked with pain from cancer and bed sores. Or perhaps easy and difficult were arising and passing, like the falling maple leaf shows front and back.

Twelve centuries earlier in China, Layman P'ang cried out, "Difficult, difficult, difficult, like trying to scatter ten measures of sesame seed all over a tree!"

"Easy, easy, easy," returned Mrs. P'ang, as would any true Zen partner, "just like touching your feet to the ground when you get out of bed."

"Neither difficult nor easy," one-upped Ling-chao, their dutiful daughter, going beyond her parents, "on the tips of the hundred grasses, the Ancestors' meaning."

ZEN IS DIFFICULT, DIFFICULT, DIFFICULT because *we* are difficult. One important strand in our great difficulty is our seemingly insatiable desire for our lives to be something other than they are. This is the realm of the *hungry ghost,* one of the psychological territories we all travel through. When we are hungry ghosts, it is as if our mouths, eyes, and bellies are big, while our necks are small, not allowing that which we consume to be digested. Pure water turns into fire, pus, or blood as we attempt to drink. We can wander in circles in this realm for long periods, continuing the struggle to satisfy our desire by chasing after some *thing,* despite all the mounting evidence that points to the inherent inability of any *thing* to ever truly satisfy, and to the truth that we are addicted to the process of the chase rather than to the object of our desire.

In Zen training the hungry ghost realm also presents as the attempt to *"get"* emptiness. "I needed so much to have nothing to touch," sings Leonard Cohen, "I've always been greedy this way."

AS A YOUNG MAN I was equally greedy for some*one* to touch. I once came to dokusan (a one-on-one private encounter with a Zen teacher) and confided to Roshi, "I'm not getting enough sex. I want sex almost all the time. One of the *Great Vows* says, 'Desires are inexhaustible, I vow to end them.' There seems to be no end of this at all."

Roshi looked at me with concern. "Because desires are inexhaustible, we vow to end them. If desires weren't inexhaustible, there'd be no need to vow. Do you understand?"

I didn't understand.

WHAT I UNDERSTAND NOW is that we tell ourselves all kinds of stories—about wanting to be in bed with our lover, or, like Katagiri Roshi, about not wanting to be in bed with death—and we construct a self from a self-told story of what we are not getting or of what we have that we wish we didn't. In this, we unconsciously hope to avoid the utter transience of it all. We reify a subject who sees, hears, smells, tastes, touches, and thinks—*especially* thinks. "I didn't get the childhood I wanted." "I'm not doing the work I want." "I don't have the community I want." "I don't want this breaking-down-old-skin bag to be a breaking-down-old-skin bag." What are the stories you use to create a suffering self?

Fortunately, this process of fixing a self is difficult to maintain. The great universe chews up everything and reconfigures it, like my eleven-year-old son playing with Legos—building blocks that he puts together and pulls apart in elaborate and seemingly infinite (and often horrific) combinations. Trying to maintain one Lego configuration, one story of a self, is like trying to attach ten measures of sesame seeds to a tree. It just doesn't work.

Nevertheless, we walk through repetitive cycles, recreating past patterns in work, relationship, and meditation, yearning to *get it*—get it right, get it all, get it done, as if "getting it" could quench our thirsting desire. We sometimes take this wanting-to-get stance even when we are aware that "getting" won't lead to satisfaction, knowing that the getting stance will lead to suffering. Katagiri Roshi likened this to a yak licking its tail, continuing even after its tongue bleeds, because at least when licking and bleeding, the yak has some feeling and is distracted for a while from the truth of its mind-numbing circumstances.

Living a Zen lifestyle, with all its routines and rituals, can be co-opted into our efforts to numb ourselves from the pain of this life. Zen students sometimes trudge through the daily schedule like old yaks feeding on a mountain. At such a time, we may be good yaks, yaks living out someone else's agenda, but yaks nonetheless, missing the dynamic potential of human beings.

Another misuse of Zen practice is to adopt the stance of trying to "get" Zen. Many times I've heard students complain, "I just don't *get* Zen." No one in fifteen years of teaching has come to the dokusan room and said, "I just don't *give* Zen."

"Giving" not "getting" is the first of the six perfections and giving spiritual gifts is considered to be the antidote to the hungry ghost realm. Dogen Zenji, the thirteenth-century founder of Japanese Soto, gives it up like this: "To give to yourself is a part of giving. To give to your family is also giving." Dogen goes on to encourage us to celebrate our own acts of giving even really tiny gifts because through acts of generosity we enter the merit-stream of the buddhas by acting like enlightening beings.

"Getting," though, is not the enemy. When we give the love we want, we get the love we want. When we give zazen to zazen, we realize zazen together. When we give the way to the way, we attain the way. Therefore, in the traditional chant before receiving a meal we say, "May we, with all living beings, realize the emptiness of the three wheels: giver, *receiver,* and gift."

Yet, there is significance in how we spin the wheel. While "getting Zen" relies on our continued looking away, depending on someone else to hand us Zen, "giving Zen" is an approach to our life through which we can take responsibility and manifest freedom from self-clinging. We can turn our lives around again (and again) from devoting our awareness to what we are not getting, to living a creative life of giving. However, this turning can be difficult and counterintuitive, like turning to walk upstream toward the source of heart through the current of our habit patterns pushing us the other way.

When my daughter was eight, she commented on her soccer team saying, "We haven't won any games and I haven't scored a goal yet."

"Well," I said in a fatherly tone, "you know, winning isn't the most important thing." Then just for fun I asked, "What is the most important thing?"

"ME," she said without hesitation; and for an eight-year-old this is probably dead on.

For a thirty-, forty-, or fifty-year-old, however, that response would be dead off. For us, realizing that success or failure is not me, not mine, not the self (while simultaneously taking full responsibility for our actions), we are filled with ease and joy.

With training, we can turn ourselves around. Ego, however, is pernicious and persistent. Fluency in Zen practice can lead tail-licking Zen students to feel real by attaching to and identifying with the difficulty of our undertaking. Please allow Mrs. P'ang to enter: "Easy, easy, easy, just like touching our feet to the ground when you get out of bed."

On the other hand, if you are making a nest in "easy," you might turn your attention to the true meaning of the Ancestors. There is no evidence that those in the past who were attached to an easy-going way transmitted the Dharma to those dependent on them (namely, to us) in the present.

To the contrary, in Dogen's "Universally Recommended Instructions for Zazen," often chanted after evening zazen, we find:

Consider the Buddha: although he was wise at birth, the traces of his six years of upright sitting can yet be seen. As for Bodhidharma, although he had received the mind-seal, his nine years of facing a wall is celebrated still. Even if the ancient sages were like this, how can we today dispense with wholehearted practice?

HOW CAN WE REALIZE THE ANCESTORS' MEANING? How can we hold to wholehearted practice? How can we actually live a life of giving? We can begin by giving our word, vowing again and again (no matter how often we fall down) to carry all beings to the Other Shore, from the shore of suffering to the shore of liberation, to cut off the mind road, to pass through all Dharma gates, and to embrace the way of Buddha. Vowing like this is pure wanting, wholehearted wanting, wanting without a self-limited outcome.

Practically speaking, vowing can be given life by getting out of bed and sitting zazen in the morning, quietly cultivating a generous mind, giving attention to the "tips of the hundred grasses"—the seeing, hearing, tasting, smelling, touching, thinking of the moment at hand. Not sticking onto any of it as me, myself, or mine—giving up our "self" project. Instead, giving body and mind to the Buddha way, precisely devoting ourselves to the practice given us. We can raise our voices with the *Heart Sutra* and then give away all the merit generated to the truth of the liberation of all living beings. We can eat our breakfast with our family or alone, giving our awareness to all the guests that arise and pass. Throughout the day, we can give up our habit of constantly placing our fleeting selves in the starring role in the drama of life.

In "Thunder on the Mountain," Bob Dylan sings, "gonna forget about myself for a while / and go out and see what others need."

At just such a time, life isn't about getting, the meaning of Zen is given, and there is really nothing to worry about.

2. Just a Question about Technique: Wall or No Wall?

A student asked, "When you practice zazen facing a wall, are you actually supposed to be looking at it?"

Katagiri Roshi responded, "No. The wall is there but the wall is not there."

Sounding irritated, the student tried again, "This is just a question about technique. Are you supposed to focus on the wall?"

Katagiri Roshi said, "No. If you focus on the wall, at that time you observe the wall. Just sit down without wall or no-wall."

IN DECEMBER OF 1978 I sat my first *sesshin*, a week-long retreat of intensive meditation. This one was the Rohatsu sesshin commemorating the Buddha's enlightenment. I spent the week with Katagiri Roshi facing a wall for seven days. The schedule was grueling. After sitting in a lotus pose most of the morning from before 5:00 a.m. until breakfast ended at 7:45 a.m., we had about twenty minutes to use the toilet and have tea. "A schedule so tight that there isn't time to take a shit," remarked a friend. We were back in the zendo, the meditation hall, by 8:15 and again had a twenty-minute break at about 12:45 p.m. The only time during the day other than meals that we turned inward from facing the wall was during the morning Dharma talk that could last as long as two hours.

Katagiri Roshi's resolute buoyancy while following the schedule together with us captivated me so completely that I continued to train with him until his death in 1990. However, in 1978 my knees and spirit were in no shape for such a workout. I've often thought back to this first sesshin and wondered what Roshi had talked about—I couldn't remember a single word! Apparently, I was in too much turmoil ("Your mind threw up," he told me afterward) to store anything he had said. Then recently I discovered that the Minnesota Zen Center had issued CDs of many of Katagiri Roshi's talks and I was delighted to find that the Rohatsu sesshin of 1978 was among them.

Listening to my old master's teaching again has been a delight. I have been struck time and again by the clear joy in the tone of his voice as well as the depth of his teaching. For example, Roshi once explained the phrase from Dogen, "*sanzen* is zazen." Commonly this phrase is translated as "Zen practice is zazen." However, Roshi believed that the character for *san* wasn't conveyed by "practice." Instead, he translated *san* as "to surrender" or "to submit." Practicing Zen as *sanzen* meant surrendering oneself fully, giving—all the thoughts and feelings, all our grasping for an identity—to the very form of sitting itself.

Roshi went on to translate *zen* as "manifesting tranquility or simplicity." *Sanzen* in this light means to "surrender to the manifestation of tranquility" or to "submit to the demonstration of simplicity." This zazen as sanzen requires an unconditional surrender, witness consciousness included. There can be no fight with the person doing it. A student sitting and *observing* the wall as a subject observing an object would not be sanzen.

The student in the above story ran into the wall of Katagiri's "No," complemented by, "The wall is there but the wall is not there." Roshi, by pulling out the pins of dualistic zazen, abruptly offers us Buddha's zazen. Throughout his teaching career, Katagiri Roshi urged us to just wholeheartedly surrender. Doing zazen in this way itself conveys simplicity, demonstrates tranquility. Katagiri Roshi's Zen was an *activity* (in contrast to vogue Zen that emphasizes private mental experience), a presentation of Buddha nature, certainly not sitting and sleeping.

I'm struck today by Roshi's wholehearted zazen and his use of "surrender" or "submission." These words don't harmonize well with contemporary American Zen. A Google search for "zazen" (that which is sanzen) calls up paid advertisements for "Meditate in Comfort" and "Zazen for Sale." The first site I check gives this definition of zazen with five personal possessive pronouns, "Zazen is the practice of awareness, of bringing your attention, or concentration, to the present moment—this whole and complete moment— by bringing your awareness to your posture, your breathing, and your state of mind."

This is a self-centered zazen of "me," "myself," and "I." A zazen of a person and a wall, a dualistic process of "you" bringing "your" awareness to something. Even bringing your attention to a "whole and complete moment" is already living a divided life, you facing a wall, an earthworm cut in two.

My concern about sanzen in America escalated recently when two friends, prominent second-generation American Zen teachers, told me in separate conversations that they were not training students the way their teachers trained them. "If I tried," said one, "every one would leave and we have a big mortgage payment every month."

Talking with my friends, I also confessed that in my first teaching position, I often felt the weight of large revenue projections restraining my decisions about who and what to teach and subtly influencing what and who not to teach. Would fifty people have shown up for class if I taught zazen as submission? Probably not.

When we package the Dharma in a flashy box with no contents, we offer only the skin of Dharma. It might be better for authentic Dharma to die than to establish large groups and spew out teachers regurgitating sound bites like those that sell special transient mind-states as the Buddha mind.

However, in order to communicate and spread the Dharma more widely—and in order for us leaders of Buddhist centers to make our budgeted revenues—we Dharma teachers may be slipping into a self-centered inversion of what first generation teachers like Katagiri Roshi offered to us such a short time ago.

If future generations are to actualize the skin, muscle, bones, and marrow of surrendering to tranquility, then how we define and practice sanzen is critical. Define and practice sanzen in a limited way—because of our limited understanding or by our needs for fame and gain—and we will limit what Zen practice becomes in this country.

The shine from the skin of the glossy ads in today's Buddhist journals may be already blinding our vision so much that we may have already irrevocably retrofitted Zen as a commodity for high-end consumption and thereby gentrified Zen to meld with contemporary faddish notions of psychological correctness, and of *I* and *Thou*.

However, compromising principles in order to survive and thrive is not new in Zen history. Steven Heine in *Zen Skin, Zen Marrow: Will the Real Zen Buddhism Please Stand Up?* summarizes scholarly research that has led to a deconstruction of the myth of Zen. Both in China and Japan, Zen masters appear to have colluded with powerful regimes, including the wanton maligning of Zen training and philosophy to enhance Japanese imperial and colonial ambitions before and during World War II. Perhaps in the West we can give this tradition a fresh start, mindful of our predecessors' strengths *and* weaknesses.

In the little basement zendo where I now train and teach, we've returned to chanting the sutra that opens the Dharma talk in both Japanese and English, rather than only in English. Chanting the way that I trained with Katagiri Roshi, I now find myself intensely interested in the quiet space, the inhalation that marks the transition from Japanese to English. This pivot point, a full dynamic stop, marks the transmission of Zen from East to West.

It is essential to urgently sit here, without a wall and without no-wall, appreciating and honoring those who came before us so that there may be those who come after us.

3. The Dynamic Working of Realization

Katagiri Roshi growled, "Pick up the newspaper!"

"T HE THOROUGH CLARIFICATION of birth and death is the Buddha family's single great matter." This sentence begins "The Meaning of Practice and Verification" *("Shushogi"),* a short essay composed of bits and pieces of Dogen's *Shobogenzo* selected by a group of Soto Zen priests about one hundred years ago. These priests were intent on simply and clearly expressing the essence of our school, and did such a fine job that their work continues to be studied, chanted, and sung in Japan and in the West.

Notice here that the single great matter is not about creating or discovering a meaning or explanation for birth and death. The single great matter is simply clarifying the *"What?"* That is, *what* is birth and death in this vividly hopping-along moment?

How can we thoroughly clarify that which is hopping along? "When birth comes," says Dogen Zenji in "Birth and Death"

(*"Shoji"*), "face and actualize birth, and when death comes, face and actualize death."

To live and die like this requires fearlessness and invites a fearless practice like zazen. When we sit in the repose of Buddha, in the stability and harmony of the upright pose, we live and die completely with the expansion and contraction of the belly with each breath. In our life off the cushion, thorough clarification continues when we act, speak, and think congruently with the delicate truth that everything is coming together and passing away as we act, speak, and think.

A FRIEND who studies Tibetan Buddhism told me a story about a married couple who came to Atisha, a great Indian adept who played a pivotal role in transmitting the Dharma to Tibet. They asked him to make his teaching more practical. "For example," the woman said, "we fight all the time. If I say it's this, he says it's that. How can the Buddha's teaching help us be free from fighting?"

"When you notice that you are getting into a fight," said Atisha, "preface your bitter words with 'You who will die soon.' For example, 'You who will die soon, go milk the yak.'"

This straightforward medicine, awareness of the fleeting quality of this ephemeral life in the midst and context of the mundane, apparently helped the couple live more happily together and got the yak milked too.

Leonard Cohen, in "Here It Is," takes up another perspective, fearlessly wishing for birth and death to be birth and death.

May everyone live
And may everyone die.

16

No dread or judgment here about death. Because each of us lives, a warm-hearted wish for it to be so. Because each of us dies, a warm-hearted wish for it to be so. And because meeting will end in parting: hello, good-bye.

But let's not wallow in idealism either. When love comes, rejoice. When love leaves, cry. This too is just arising and passing. This too can be faced and entered into fully when we embrace love's arrival *and* departure as the life of Buddha.

Ego, though, and our thinking about entering into birth and death or not can cause us to hold back, missing the opportunity of birth and death that is us, right now. We can hide behind a tree and remain in the watcher position for a long time.

During our nonresidential practice periods at the Minnesota Zen Center, students took turns giving talks at 4:30 a.m. Roshi usually sat very quietly with his inverted half-moon mouth, a world-class frown, and very seldom made any comment about our wobbly efforts to express the Dharma. One morning Roy, a long-time student of Katagiri Roshi, began his talk verbally stumbling around.

> While I was walking to the zendo I began crossing the street just as a piece of newspaper was picked up by the wind and blown across my path. As I bent down to pick up the paper, I thought, "I hope someone sees me bending down to pick up this paper," so I froze. I didn't want to pick up the newspaper for the wrong reason. I could see how stinky my ego was, only wanting to do something small for the good if someone saw me doing it. Then I noticed that no one else was around, so I started chasing the paper, but just as I bent down to grab it, I thought, "*I* will still know that *I'm* doing

something good, so picking it up is still stinky." I didn't know what to do. By this time, the newspaper had blown away, so I gave up.

Out of the silence, Roshi growled, "Pick up the newspaper!"

Jumping into birth and death, picking up the newspaper, is the dynamic working of realization. What must be dropped to actualize this dynamic working now?

4. We Don't Study Koans

"Roshi," I asked, "do we study koans?"

"No," responded Roshi.

"Hmm," I said. "Well, you often give lectures on koans and you often comment on Dogen commenting on koans, so couldn't we say that we do study koans, in a way?"

"No," responded Roshi strongly and with irritation. "No, we don't study koans!"

IN THE MODERN ZEN WORLD there are at least two approaches to letting go of body and mind: *shikantaza* (which we could translate as, "earnest, vivid sitting") and working with the Mu koan *(muji)* along with successive koan training. Shikantaza is usually associated with the Soto school while koan training is associated with the Rinzai school. In both the past and present, however, the distinction has not been so neat. The medieval Soto school created an extensive collection of koan commentaries that were an integral aspect of the transmission throughout the period that reflect a distinctive approach to koan training. Presently, one of the most vital lines in Soto Zen, those descended from Daiun Harada, use a modified version of the Rinzai koan curriculum.

Zen teachers from both schools sometimes emphasize the differences in these two practices. One contemporary koan teacher suggested, for instance, that shikantaza was for people who enjoyed living under the tyranny of their high school basketball coach (i.e., it's for people who like to be controlled). On the other hand, my own master, Dainin Katagiri Roshi, seemed to admire the Rinzai spirit but occasionally spoke disparagingly of koan Zen. He regarded muji as groping for spiritual experience. "How can you manifest peace and harmony while fighting with Mu?"

However, students and teachers of these two approaches to Zen are mixing in America. Students from shikantaza centers like the San Francisco Zen Center move freely to centers with koan-trained teachers such as Great Vow Zen Monastery or Zen Mountain Monastery and vice versa. Zen teachers from the two approaches are also interacting, perhaps more than has been the case for some time, and mixing shikantaza and koan training. One shikantaza-trained teacher, for example, has put together a collection of thirty koans that he uses with students.

The koan tradition developed in China during the later centuries of the first millennia. The word *koan* was borrowed from the legal system where it referred to a definitive ruling, a public case. Just as a judge was qualified to discern and present the public case involving a criminal matter, so Zen masters were considered qualified to present a definitive judgment regarding matters of enlightenment. Likewise, just as the duty of the judge was to settle a dispute between two parties following the principle of fairness, so the Zen master, in the truth-happening moment presented by the koan, settled the matter of the sacred, within the mundane, or vice versa, also following the principle of fairness, without favoring either the sacred or the mundane.

In addition, it is important to appreciate the belief in the tradition that through contemplating the koan, the practitioner could enter into the same quality of mind as the master who had originally uttered the turning words of the koan.

In a similar manner, Dogen Zenji regarded shikantaza as the wondrous method of Buddhas and ancestors, relying on no particular word. Dogen's attitude toward words, and "turning words" (key phrases within koans that have the potential to turn the hearer toward enlightenment) specifically, was expressed in one of his commentaries on Baizhang's Wild Fox:

> If you assert that a turning word by an outsider can liberate a wild fox then there must be innumerable turning words by mountains, rivers, and the great earth from the incalculable past . . . . To say that the current Baizhang's turning words alone liberate the wild fox is to deny the way of the ancestors. To say that mountains, rivers, and the great earth have never uttered a single turning word is to say that there is no place for the current Baizhang to even open his mouth.

During my years of Zen practice and teaching, I've had opportunities to explore shikantaza and koans with some really fine teachers and students. In the remainder of this chapter I explore similarities and differences between shikantaza and koan training by sharing some stories and offering some provisional conclusions about what I've learned.

DURING THE THIRTEEN YEARS 1977–90 I studied with the Soto master Dainin Katagiri Roshi at the Minnesota Zen Center. Katagiri

Roshi was vigilant in his focus on transmitting the Zen of Dogen Zenji which he understood as shikantaza, or as he might have put it, "not-a-technique zazen." Roshi generally reserved his role as judge for those teachers or students he saw as using zazen like a vending machine, putting in the coin of effort and expecting some immediate reward.

"In Rinzai Zen," Katagiri Roshi once said, "they sit with many questions, many koans. In Soto Zen we have just one big koan, so called *shikantaza,* so-called *genjokoan* (the koan of 'actualizing the fundamental point')."

In the late '70s and early '80s most people who came to Zen arrived either through reading Suzuki Roshi's *Zen Mind, Beginner's Mind,* or Kapleau Roshi's *Three Pillars of Zen.* Those who came by way of *Zen Mind, Beginner's Mind,* with its implicit, "everyday mind is the way" orientation, often seemed determined to attain nonattainment. Those, like me, who came by way of *Three Pillars of Zen,* with its many stories of remarkable breakthrough experiences by way of muji, were confused and disappointed that Katagiri Roshi offered no muji, no koan. "Dogen's Zen," Katagiri Roshi often said, "gives no sweet candy."

No-sweet-candy Zen resonated for many stolid middle-class Minnesotans who didn't think they deserved sweet candy anyway. However, as a lower-class boy from the swamps of northern Minnesota, I often felt rather out of place. I'd already experience plenty of austerity and I hungered for delicious spiritual experience.

After I'd studied for a couple years at the Zen center, I was given the job of responding to requests for information. Usually the job involved simply sending a newsletter. Occasionally a person would ask a question about Zen. As I wasn't qualified to answer such a question, I would ask Katagiri Roshi what I should say. One day I received a letter asking if we studied koans at the center. I brought the letter with me to Roshi's study.

I found Roshi sitting in seiza as usual at his Japanese-style desk, glasses perched on his nose, studying a sutra. "Roshi," I asked, "do we study koans?"

"No," responded Roshi, lining up with the Soto Zen orthodoxy.

"Hmm," I said, not wanting to chase an interested person away from our small and struggling group by giving him an answer that I guessed he did not want. "Well, you do often give lectures on koans, and you often comment on Dogen commenting on koans, so couldn't we say that we do study koans?"

I was often inspired and intrigued by Roshi's commentaries on the koans from *The Blue Cliff Record* and by the koans themselves. I was also hoping for Roshi to affirm my own interest in koans.

"No," responded Roshi strongly and with irritation. "No, we don't study koans!"

We didn't study koans in the manner of tracing certain turning words uttered by the ancients back to their origin so that we could experience the same mind as the ancients. Nor did Katagiri Roshi place himself in the position of the judge for someone's spiritual life. And thus I set aside my interest in koans and devoted myself to shikantaza because I wanted to study Zen with Katagiri Roshi and for him shikantaza was shikantaza and koans were koans.

Shikantaza was not an easy practice because I was not clear about what shikantaza was. Zazen *had* seemed clear in the beginning of my training, when Katagiri Roshi told me to "just be one with the breath." After I could follow the breath for longer periods, especially in sesshin, he told me that shikantaza wasn't following the breath. "Don't be attached to anything," he admonished me.

Practicing "not-being-attached-to-anything" confused me. If we don't get from practice anything we can keep, why bother? And if there is something to get, why not go after it directly? Apparently, I wasn't alone in my confusion. At the end of the last work period at a practice period at Hokyoji, the Minnesota Zen Center's rustic monastery in southeastern Minnesota, I found myself walking to the workshop with an armload of garden tools with one of Roshi's oldest students, Roy. We had just three periods of zazen left after weeks of many periods of zazen each day.

Roy had begun his practice with Suzuki Roshi in the early '60s and had followed Katagiri Roshi from California to Minnesota despite Katagiri telling all of his California students not to follow him to Minnesota. I admired Roy for coming anyway. "How are you doing, Roy?" I asked.

"Oh, well," Roy began by stumbling into words gradually as was his style. "Well, you know, um, I've got just, um . . . um, well, three sittings to understand what I'm doing."

Twenty years of shikantaza and he doesn't know what he's doing? I had been studying for six or seven years at the time and shikantaza still seemed like a mirage of water on the road ahead, but I was holding out hope that if I continued long enough I'd eventually get something that I could hold on to (this despite the hundreds of Dharma talks and dokusans with Katagiri Roshi teaching the ungraspability of *all* phenomena).

As it happened, Roshi offered practice-period-ending dokusan that afternoon. As I came into the dokusan room, I was delighted to see how bright and relaxed Roshi seemed.

"Roshi," I inquired, feeling a very open-hearted connection with him, "what *exactly* is shikantaza?"

"Zen practice," he said, "is not something particular."

Now I see that the blessing of shikantaza lies here. If shikantaza isn't anything particular, it isn't possible to do it right—nor is it possible to do it wrong. Shikantaza isn't limited by correct and incorrect.

Even though shikantaza isn't about getting anything particular, I did find that given considerable "wholehearted effort without figuring" and wise guidance from Katagiri Roshi, delicious breakthrough experiences were possible. Indeed, with ideas broken, shikantaza is deliciousness itself—what Dogen Zenji called self-enjoyment samadhi.

AFTER KATAGIRI ROSHI DIED IN 1990, I began a dozen years of studying koans with various teachers. I settled for a while at Bukkokuji, a small temple hidden in a crag behind the Obama train station a few blocks from the Japan Sea. My first koan teacher was Bukkokuji's abbot for thirty-some years, Tangen Harada Roshi. Tangen Roshi was the only (of sixty-some) surviving direct successor of the famous Daiun Harada Roshi. Daiun Harada Roshi had been adopted by a temple—the same Bukkokuji I found out later—when he was a young boy and was eventually ordained as a Soto Zen priest. Later, disappointed with the quality of training in Soto Zen, Daiun Harada Roshi entered training at a Rinzai monastery, completed koan training and received *inka* (literally, the "legitimate seal of clearly furnished proof" of enlightenment). He is widely credited for bringing muji and koan training back into the Soto school.

More than a century after Daiun Harada's practice at Bukkokuji, the group of practitioners consisted of about fifteen Japanese monks (mostly outsiders who didn't care much about their careers as monks; since Bukkokuji wasn't a recognized training monastery their time at Bukkokuji wouldn't count for the training certificate needed to run their own temple), fifteen Westerners (former drug dealers, broken-hearted lovers, terminal introverts, hostile outcasts, and Zen tourists like myself), and a few hunchbacked, elderly women from the neighborhood (of unimpeachable character).

Bukkokuji also served as a dining hall for many stray cats that flocked in from all over town to eat leftover rice mixed with bonito, the dried-fish flakes popular in Japanese cuisine. This was because a monk nicknamed the Cat Monk put out food for the cats after the human's evening meal. Tangen Roshi forbade buying cat food but allowed the bonito. Thus, cats were thick as thieves at Bukkokuji, and thieves they were, regularly probing my room and stealing the contraband croissants I smuggled in from the only Western-style bakery in town. Maybe because he had been homeless before Tangen Roshi picked him up at a train station and brought him to Bukkokuji, the Cat Monk had strong affection for the homeless cats.

After I had been in residence for a week or two, Tangen Roshi gave a talk in which he summarized the various approaches to letting go of body and life.

You are here already pouring heart and soul into just this one-doing. Ahhhh! Muji-one-doing-one-doing-muji! You are entrusting everything to Mu, giving everything to Mu. Please, give everything. There is no side track, no time to look away.

The next time I met with Tangen Roshi in dokusan, he urged me to take up muji. "Muji," he said, "is like a machete—*uuuhaaah!*" he cried as he swung his *kyosaku,* the famous Zen awakening stick, powerfully demonstrating his point. Holding the kyosaku again with both hands he continued, "Shikantaza is letting go of everything," as both hands vigorously opened and the kyosaku bounced on the tatami.

I told Tangen Roshi—feeling guilty about doing something that Katagiri Roshi may not have approved of—that I wanted to take up muji. *Finally, I might get something out of this,* I thought to myself, only half kidding.

"Oh, you do?" Tangen Roshi seemed surprised.

"Yes, what do I do?" I asked, wanting to get the whole scoop.

"Okay, you know Joshu Zenji, neh? Joshu Zenji was once asked by a monk, 'Does a cat have Buddha nature?' Oh, not cat—I mean *dog.* Okay? Too many cats here. So ' . . . does a cat have Buddha nature?' Oh, no, I mean *dog*—doesn't matter, neh? Joshu answered, 'Muuuuuuu.' You must become this 'Mu.'"

Katagiri Roshi's initial instruction was to become one with the breath and Tangen Roshi advised me to begin muji by becoming one with Mu. Tangen Roshi's presentation style was also reminiscent of Katagiri Roshi's—cats and dogs were all mixed up and it didn't seem to matter which was which.

So I set to work with Mu. I soon learned that almost everyone at Bukkokuji was working with Mu, including monks who had been training with Tangen Roshi for fifteen years. The lore at Bukkokuji was that no one had yet "passed" Mu, that Tangen Roshi's muji-one-doing-one-doing-muji was not about getting something particular. Thus, the standard way of meeting Tangen Roshi in dokusan was to intone Mu then say *"Muji ni sanjite orimasu"* (in English, "I vow to practice Mu timelessly").

Some monastics, especially the newly arrived Westerners, would present Mu so loudly that it could be heard throughout the monastery, like cows bleating in the early morning. Their dokusan sessions were especially short. Mu for me was almost always very quiet so when I presented Mu to Tangen Roshi it would be almost as soft as a breath. Noticing the difference between my presentation and what I heard from the dokusan line, I asked Tangen Roshi if I was doing Mu correctly. "Ahhhhh, no one right Mu," he said in his coarse English. "You do shikantaza for long time . . . so of course, Mu is very quiet."

Although Tangen Roshi taught Mu as ungraspable, encouraging us to practice Mu timelessly, the diligence and wholeheartedness of the practitioners at Bukkokuji was remarkable. There was seldom even a short period of time, twenty-four hours of the day, in or out of sesshin, when the zendo was empty. A monk who came to Bukkokuji from a nearby Rinzai temple for every sesshin and who happened to be assigned a seat next to me, exemplified that wholeheartedness by sitting zazen through every break. He was always sitting when I went to bed and was always sitting when I got up. I didn't see him nod off once during zazen. One of my friends claimed to have seen him lie down—once.

After nine months at Bukkokuji, humbled by the deep practice I saw around me and with categories shaken as to what distinguished Soto from Rinzai as well as shikantaza from koan, I returned to Minneapolis.

A FEW YEARS LATER I was teaching Zen. During this period I taught that shikantaza was muji and muji was shikantaza. One experience that helped free me from this particular view was a Dharma encounter with a waitress. I was meeting with some old Minnesota Zen Center friends at the Lotus Vietnamese Restaurant in the Uptown area of Minneapolis. The server, a hip-looking, probably over-educated, underemployed artist with long white shiny legs, overheard our conversation. "Are you talking about *Dharma?*" she asked with some excitement.

"Yes," I said, reluctant to include her in our conversation.

"What strand?" she asked. "What strand of Dharma?"

"No strand," I said, feeling a sudden surge of excitement at the opportunity to have a Dharma encounter at the Lotus Restaurant.

She turned and faced me directly, dropping her bubbly presentation, tipping her head forward so that she looked over the top of her purple horn-rimmed glasses as she looked me up and down. After a pause she said, "What strand of no strand?"

"How could no strand have a strand?" I replied, confident of victory.

"That's enough," she said with frustration, "I have a headache. I'm going for a smoke. I'll send someone else to wait on you," she called over her shoulder.

Clearly, I was defeated. Sometimes cats and dogs can be mixed up, but sometimes it is best to call a cat a cat and a dog and dog. Sometimes shikantaza is shikantaza and muji is muji.

TEN YEARS after Tangen Roshi urged me to work with muji and several years after my defeat by the waitress at the Lotus, I participated in a couple of sesshins on Whidbey Island with Shodo Harada Roshi, a wonderful Rinzai master. When I entered his one-to-one meeting room, I found Shodo Harada Roshi had the strongest presence of no-one-being-present that I had ever felt. After I gave him the highlights of my spiritual resumé—what practices I'd done with whom, what insights I'd had and how they had impacted daily life—I asked him for practice instructions. He gave me a koan that doesn't belong to any system, saying that he wanted to work with me outside of categories. "I know a little about the Daiun Harada Roshi approach," I said, "but what specific suggestions for working with this do you recommend?"

"Zen practice," he said, "is not something particular."

I was so happy to hear this.

AT THE BEGINNING OF MY PRACTICE shikantaza was shikantaza and koans were koans. Then in the middle years, shikantaza was koans and koans were shikantaza. Now after almost thirty years of shikantaza and koan practice and fifteen years as a teacher, I find myself back at the beginning. Shikantaza is shikantaza and koans are koans.

What else have I found? First, I'm pretty certain that delicious morsels are available through muji *and* shikantaza. It largely depends upon how they are taught, on our relationship with the teacher who offers them to us, and how we receive and vigorously become shikantaza or muji.

Second, the morsels don't matter nearly as much as I originally believed. Morsels can be important, can even be the most important thing for a while, but that isn't due to the nature of the morsels since they have none. Whether morsels are important or not depends on whether they are actualized in how we live or not.

Third, I'm also pretty certain that Zen practice—including shikantaza and muji—is not something particular. Shikantaza and koans, Soto and Rinzai, the Cat Monk and the waitress, you and I— each thing has the wondrous power to be free from itself. As such, everything is broken, not even able to carry itself. Thus, our bodies and our lives are already free.

Anyway, we don't study koans.

5. Already You Are Stuck

"How can 'I' go beyond self-consciousness?" I asked.
Katagiri Roshi said, "Already you are stuck."

WE MAY NOT STUDY KOANS but investigating the subject/object split, the mysterious pivot of suffering and nirvana is the lifeblood of Soto Zen training.

Beginning with my early tastes of deep quiet a couple years after I began to practice Zen, and contrary to my expectation of the "self" dropping away, I experienced the separation of self and other growing more vividly clear. The more I quieted down, the more distinct the "I" became who was "having" this experience. In addition, the "I" seemed to grow, incorporating all sights, sounds, smells, tastes, touches, and thoughts.

One day I brought this problem up with Katagiri Roshi. "You must go beyond self-consciousness," he said.

Caught short, I asked, "How can 'I' go beyond self-consciousness?"

"When you sit, just sit. When you bow, just bow."

Because he had said this same thing many times, and because that was what I had been trying to do for several years, his reply added to my frustration. The question, though, "How to go beyond self-consciousness?" flowed out of my mouth and hit me hard.

Roshi explained the "found koan" in the context of the famous meeting of the Sixth Ancestors in China and Nanyueh, in which the Sixth Ancestor, Hui-neng, asked, "What is it that thus comes?"

The "what?" in "What is it that thus comes?" informs and inspires Soto practice still and is the vital way of earnest, vivid sitting. Zazen as *"What?"* cuts through and overturns distinctions between calming the mind and discerning the real (or, to use traditional terms, *shamatha* and *vipassana*).

KATAGIRI ROSHI'S SECOND TEACHER, Hashimoto Eko Roshi, taught the importance of the bodily process of wholehearted inquiry or what might be called "Great Doubt" in the Rinzai school. For instance, in his commentary on Dogen Zenji's teaching on the Way-Seeking Mind, Hashimoto Roshi wrote,

The easiest way to enter the Buddha Way is gradually to go to the heart of the Buddha Way from this kind of upright poem (i.e., Dogen's fascicle "Way-Seeking Mind"). It is important to stick it on your body to really appreciate it. Even though it is simple, don't be rash . . . if you gradually appreciate these words and carry them to temples as if these words are something simple, then you will realize that in reality it has a deep, penetrating meaning without reward. It is guaranteed that if you read it well and carry this real truth on pilgrimage you will finally realize the inner truth of the Buddha Way.

32

IN MY CASE the simple poem without reward that stuck to my body became, "How can I go beyond self-consciousness?"

After this question found me, I discovered that Dogen Zenji addressed the issue of going beyond the self in many places. Considering the Wild Fox koan where a Zen master falls into the body of a fox for five hundred years, Dogen questions, " . . . Just what is the subject that falls and just what is the object that is fallen into?"

In response, Dogen turns the question and brings it back home: "What form and color does the universe that has continued from the past have in the present?"

Or more simply put, *what* is the self? *What* is the other?

Hearing Katagiri Roshi's phrase, "go beyond self-consciousness," I began a period of several years, which seemed like five hundred lifetimes, during which I was haunted and taunted by the issue of the nature of subject and object. Virtually every time I quieted down in zazen, or in a still moment while walking around Lake Calhoun, or while driving to work, the question would arise as if it had a life of its own, "How to go beyond self-consciousness?" Especially in sesshin dokusan, I would ask Roshi this question.

One day he looked at me with concerned, soft eyes. "You don't understand who you are," he said. "Before you think who you are, you are you, exactly you are you, you know?"

"No," I said, "I don't know. That's my problem."

"'Before you think who you are, you are you,' means you are exactly the universe, exactly, harmoniously intimate, no gap between. You must jump the gap between you and universe."

"How can I jump the gap?"

"With prayer."

"I am to use prayer to go beyond self-consciousness?" I asked.

I had left Catholicism and the reliance for salvation on any power outside of "me" years before and thought that the essence of Zen practice was not to rely on God or anybody.

"Yes, of course," Roshi continued, "always you are thinking, observing, calculating. This is ego. Your ego is calculating how to go beyond ego. But ego cannot go beyond ego, always holding tightly to something."

"So I should pray?"

"Yes," Roshi began to smile. "You know the story of the octopus. Japanese fishermen in old days would catch the octopus by throwing a chicken neck tied to a line into the sea. Then octopus would come and grab the chicken neck and fishermen would pull a little bit. The octopus holds on tighter. The fishermen pull more and the octopus holds on tighter. Finally, the octopus is hauled onto the fishing boat. But fishermen don't use any hooks. From the beginning the octopus is free. Let go any time, anyway."

"Okay. So I am like the octopus and I should pray. But Roshi, if there is nothing outside, no gap between me and the universe, to whom should I pray?"

"'Pray' means just pray. No object there. Just 'Help!'"

He rang the bell ending the interview. I went back to my seat in the zendo and tried silently calling "Help!" to nobody in particular. No father God with a white beard and dry ice machine appeared. At first it seemed to help because I felt more open. But soon I saw that "I" was calling "Help!" Ego calling for help with ego, hollering inside a tin can. My frustration intensified.

"How do I go beyond self-consciousness?"

SHORTLY AFTER THIS MEETING a visiting teacher from Japan, Narazaki Tsugen Roshi, arrived to lead the Rohatsu Sesshin in 1984. He was the vice-abbot of Zuioji where Roshi, Tomoe-san, Ben, Meija, and I had visited the previous year. *Finally,* I thought,

I'll be able to present my question to somebody who might be able to help me!

Narazaki Roshi was a solid and gentle man with a bright and inspiring countenance. He gave clear and simple talks. Everyone was to have only one turn at dokusan and would be allowed only one question. "No psychological questions or personal problems," we were told.

As my turn approached I was filled with energy and clarity. "How can I go beyond self-consciousness?" was cooking in my belly. I was called to go upstairs in Roshi's study, now the dokusan waiting room. My body was buzzing, trembling with energy and anticipation. "How can I go beyond self-consciousness?" I wanted to scream.

My turn finally arrived. I entered the room and was swept off my feet by the majesty and softness with which Narazaki Roshi sat, cuddled it seemed, in many layers of fine robes. My time had arrived! I did three full prostrations, sat down and asked loudly, "How can I go beyond self-consciousness?"

The translator, Katagiri Roshi's one Japanese priest, translated my question. I heard the Japanese pouring from Narazaki Roshi's mouth. *This could be it, finally!* Eagerly I waited for the English.

"Make little steps," said the translator. "Try something small like saying 'Good morning' and then say a little more when you can. Step-by-step you will overcome being self-conscious."

"What?" I stammered, then realized that the translator had misunderstood the question as a psychological, personal problem. Rather than going beyond SELF-CONSCIOUSNESS, he thought I was asking about how to get over being *self*-conscious, as in "shy."

"Oh," I said, "I think you didn't translate the question correctly." It was a bad idea to criticize the one person who could help me communicate with the venerable teacher. "I wasn't asking about self-consciousness but about going beyond the separation of self and other. Can you please ask again?"

Narazaki Roshi looked puzzled at this side conversation between the translator and me. The translator's face turned red. "No mistake. I translate what you say."

"But, please, this is my only chance, could you ask again this time about how to go beyond self and other? Do you understand?" Another error. I had assumed a superior position, trying to go beyond self and other but blundering into putting the translator down and me up. Once again, I wanted to go south but was pushing the accelerator to the floor on a northbound freeway.

At that point Narazaki Roshi broke in and he and the translator spoke briefly. I was hopeful that my question was being clarified.

"Okay," said the translator, "that's all for your turn. Please bow now and go." Narazaki Roshi reached for the bell.

"But," I protested before he could ring it, "I didn't get my question!"

"Yes, you did," said the translator, now with obvious annoyance. "Not Roshi's problem that you don't like the response."

I stomped back to the zendo fuming with anger and wallowing in judgments about arrogant Japanese Zen monks. This would not be the day for going beyond self-consciousness.

A FEW MONTHS LATER I was in dokusan again with Katagiri Roshi just half an hour before the end of another sesshin. I was tenderized and open. "How can I go beyond self-consciousness?" I asked without nearly the intensity that I often felt. In this moment, asking was simply what I did when we met.

Roshi had been sitting as usual, eyes cast down at a forty-five-degree angle, face impassive as if idling in neutral, ready to meet me.

He bolted forward, stopping just an inch from my face. "Already you are stuck!" he almost shouted.

I was startled by the uncharacteristically fierce look in his eyes. Everything stopped. He flowed backward slightly, hunched over, and then slammed his hand on the six-inch strip of carpet that separated our zabutons, staring at me all the while. Simultaneously he said in a commanding tone, "Turn over a new leaf, NOW!"

I obeyed, although writing that it was "I" who obeyed seems utterly too much and yet incomplete. Figure and ground reversed. Katagiri Roshi's bushy eyebrows obeyed. They were me. The bell ringing to end the interview obeyed—me. The tan shag carpet under my feet obeyed—me. Berk, the tender giant Zen monk sitting next to me when I returned to the zendo obeyed—me.

A new leaf had turned itself over. "There is a crack in everything," sings Leonard Cohen, "that's how the light gets in."

I had imagined that "I" could do this through my own power. Yet, the leaf didn't turn from someone else's power either. In retrospect, Roshi's phrase, "jump in with prayer," conveys it well. Whatever the words, the mysterious pivot had turned, if even for a moment. Exploring this turning point became the burning edge of my practice.

6. Clay Balls as Toilet Paper

One day while living in Yokoi Roshi's temple, Dainin-san was reading the Lotus Sutra *when he thought he was suddenly enlightened. He rushed into Yokoi Roshi's room and said, "While reading a sutra, I attained enlightenment."*

Yokoi Roshi looked up at Dainin-san and said with disgust, "How stupid you are."

Then Yokoi Roshi turned his attention back to the sutra he was studying.

ROSHI WAS ALMOST FIFTY YEARS OLD—my age today—when he helped me pick my life up and set it on a zafu. Yokoi Roshi may have thought that the young Katagiri Roshi was stupid, but to me the mature Roshi was a rough-hewed jewel.

What follows in this chapter is part of Katagiri Roshi's story as I've gleaned it from my memory of conversations with him, reminiscing with Roshi's widow, Tomoe Katagiri, and his own Dharma talks. As such, you are about to read a loosely knit collection of stories told by bystanders for their own purposes and as such are not to be relied upon in any definitive way. Digesting any tale and letting it pass through is the only way to make these dreams "definitive." One more point about my purpose: in sketching part of Katagiri Roshi's training in mid-twentieth-century Japan, my aim is to respectfully acknowledge both his brilliance and stupidity, his front and back.

Dainin-san (what I'll call the young Dainin Katagiri Roshi) began Zen training with Daicho Hayashi Roshi, a Soto Zen priest who had once traveled and taught widely but in middle age retreated to Taizoin to care for his ailing teacher and his mother. Daicho Roshi kept a copy of the I-Ching under the altar, spent much of his day studying herbal medicinal remedies (while smoking a pipe) and served as counselor/soothsayer/doctor/minister (all mixed up together) to the thirty-some families in the nearby village.

A dozen years after Dainin-san met Daicho Roshi, Tomoe-san and their very young son lived with Daicho Roshi for several months while Dainin-san was getting established in America. Tomoe-san told me that she found Daicho Roshi to be a "naturally pure monk" who didn't drink alcohol, for example, but not because it was against the precept. "Daicho Roshi just didn't drink alcohol," she said.

Daicho Roshi tried to teach Dainin-san how to live enlightenment. "When it is time to get up in the morning, just get up," Daicho Roshi often told him.

This is reminiscent of the ancient Chinese Zen poem that says: "Practice secretly, like a fool, like an idiot. If you achieve continuity, you will be the host within the host."

It wasn't until later in his life that Katagiri Roshi really appreciated the continuity of Daicho Roshi's practice. "He just lived,"

Katagiri Roshi would say. "His life was very stable, manifesting spiritual security. When I was young, I didn't understand this."

Two other teachers powerfully influenced Dainin-san. In 1948, after living with Daicho Roshi at Taizoin for only about nine months, Dainin-san was sent to Eiheiji, one of the two main monasteries of the Soto Zen school.

The world outside the monastery had changed wholly since the prewar years, millions had died, and the Americans occupied a former empire-building nation. Many Japanese felt that they had been deceived by their government, whose imperial ambitions they had recently been asked to offer their lives to support. The worldview that the Japanese had held for millennia—that they were a superior people—was challenged in every conceivable way. For Dainin-san, the fleeting quality of the world stood out in relief.

Yet the everyday life of the monks at Eiheiji was the same before and after the war. This continuity touched a deep yearning in Dainin-san. The source of that yearning Roshi believed to come from the distant past. As a small child, he had actually *eaten* incense from his family's altar. Inexplicably, Dainin-san longed for the days when the Buddha was in the world, for perfect spiritual security before consciousness could contaminate it with judgments about good and bad, right and wrong, success and failure.

At Eiheiji, with 700 years of resolute immobility, or so the story went, Dainin-san met Hashimoto Eko Roshi, one of the foremost Zen masters of twentieth-century Japan. Hashimoto Roshi was renowned for his mastery of how to live in peace and harmony in the monastic community and for returning to the ancient style of the founder of Eiheiji, Master Dogen. When Dainin-san arrived at Eiheiji, Hashimoto Roshi was the teacher in charge of training. The first instruction that Dainin-san heard from him was simple and direct: "Sit down. Become Buddha."

Dainin-san didn't understand what this meant yet upon hearing these words his heart was penetrated. His first sesshin (a more intensive variation of the usual American sesshin with wake up at about 2:00 a.m. and zazen through the day until about 10:00 p.m.) happened to be the sesshin in the twelfth month that commemorated the Buddha's enlightenment.

Dainin-san resolved to sit down and become Buddha. His body was not yet well suited for long hours of zazen. Nevertheless, he maintained the full lotus position (right foot on the left thigh, left foot on the right thigh) throughout the sesshin. Several times he passed out from the pain and knocked his head into the wall he sat facing. Senior monks would drag him out of the zendo and throw him in the snow. Dainin-san would revive, get up, come back into the zendo, and sit zazen again in the full lotus position.

How many of us have such enthusiasm for the Buddhadharma that we forsake our own comfort so completely? How many of us could forsake our own comfort without machismo, masochism, or mania but through the simple, complete joy of giving everything away for the sake of what is true?

Dainin-san's zeal must have attracted the attention of the senior monks because he was soon appointed the attendant for Hashimoto Roshi, a training opportunity that would shape his life and teaching. Years later, giving his students a taste of deep continuity through sitting down and immediately becoming Buddha became his passion. The difficulty of communicating continuity in American culture became his burden.

In ancient China, the sage Zhuangzi told of a person from the countryside who went to the city of Handan and imitated the fashionable city-style walk. But before the sage had mastered the walk of the Handan he forgot his own country way of walking, and so had to crawl home on his hands and knees.

Dainin-san wanted to learn to walk from Hashimoto Roshi. He learned that in Zen training, in every situation, the student has to understand two, three, four, five appropriate responses—otherwise, the disciple cannot fit into the teacher's life. As Hashimoto Roshi's attendant, he learned that for every action of the teacher it was his job to respond appropriately and immediately without pondering what to do. For instance, just as Hashimoto Roshi sat down it was the Dainin-san's responsibility to understand the whole situation and immediately get socks and put them on his teacher's feet. When Dainin-san didn't do this, he was scolded.

"The teacher's life is not separate from me, so I always must pay attention. Not nervously, I always have to be one with him. The point of the practice is to put us right in the middle of intimacy between you and the teacher, you and the truth, exactly."

DAININ-SAN SET OUT to learn the ancient ways of training from Hashimoto Roshi and the other senior monks. Training for the Zen monk included every action of body, speech, and thought throughout the twenty-four hours of the day. There was a proper way to perform all of the aspects of daily life—zazen, bowing, sleeping, eating, walking, speaking.

Dainin-san read Dogen Zenji's instructions for using the toilet, including first snapping your fingers three times (to alert any god-realm beings in the vicinity to move out of harm's way) and then afterward wiping your butt using small, damp clay balls about one inch in diameter—though this latter practice had not been maintained for a really long time. Dainin-san, however, did his best to follow the instructions to the letter. The other monks thought this was going too far.

I once asked Katagiri Roshi how the clay balls worked. "Pretty well," he reported, "but it was hard to find clay with the right consistency, so sometimes it was a mess. Also, it took lots of time."

Even though we might also yearn for the old ways, every Zen student finds it hard to leave his native village completely. At Eiheiji, one of the old monks always scolded the young monks who rushed about attached to their customary pace, "What are you doing? Why did you become monks—to run around?"

Then one day there was an earthquake. The ceiling, floor, walls, and pillars of the ancient monastery were all shaking. All the monks ran to get outside. As Dainin-san was running to escape the possible collapse of the building, he saw this old monk just walking steadily. A moment later as Dainin-san ran at full speed, a ceiling beam seemed to move right into his own path. He met the beam with his forehead. "No enlightenment, just pain," he joked afterward.

Nevertheless, the image of the old monk just walking like a monk, even through an earthquake, deeply impacted Dainin-san.

After three years at Eiheiji, Dainin-san walked back to Taizo-in like a monk from Eiheiji. Before he went away to Eiheiji, he would refer all questions about Zen to Daicho Roshi as he didn't know what to say. Upon returning he was startled to find that he could respond. "What happened?" he would later ask his students.

He may have left his native village. He was in danger of succeeding in his aspiration to learn to walk like a person from Handan. This is the stink of Zen.

Fortunately, Daicho Roshi then sent Dainin-san to monks' college in Tokyo. While at college, Dainin-san lived at the temple of his third teacher, Yokoi Kakudo Roshi. Katagiri Roshi would refer to him as "my friend and teacher."

Through Yokoi Roshi, Dainin-san met his wife and student of many years, Tomoe. She told me recently that Yukoi Roshi had a very strong character. He would speak directly about what was true, even in casual conversation. Tomoe-san often didn't like what Yokoi Roshi said, but even years later it was still teaching her. Yokoi Roshi's style didn't make him popular. Tomoe-san said that people would say, "'Yokoi Roshi is a sincere monk, but . . .' There is always a *but.*"

One day while living in Yokoi Roshi's temple, Dainin-san was reading the *Lotus Sutra* when he thought he was suddenly enlightened. He rushed into Yokoi Roshi's room and said, "While reading a sutra, I attained enlightenment."

Yokoi Roshi looked up at Dainin-san and said with disgust, "How stupid you are."

Then Yokoi Roshi turned his attention back to the sutra he was studying. "He always scolded me constantly. I didn't like such pain from the practice," Katagiri Roshi said later, "but now I really appreciate his way."

While he was with Yokoi Roshi, Dainin-san felt that his life, his sense of himself, was shrinking and that he might disappear. He felt like he was suffocating. One day Dainin-san asked Yokoi Roshi why he never praised, only scolded. Yokoi Roshi said, "I scold you so that you might be a normal person."

IN ADDITION TO SUFFERING through living with a teacher who always scolded him, Dainin-san didn't have enough money for college. He tried to earn some money by working at a bookstore. His first day on the job, the owner told him to keep his eye on a rack of expensive books. Sometime later, the owner happened to be passing through the shelves and found Dainin-san standing where he had left him, staring at the expensive books with his hands folded over his solar plexus, Zen monk style. "What are you doing?" he asked.

"Watching these books," said Dainin-san.

Standing in the aisle at this large Tokyo bookstore, Dainin-san had come a long way. His journey began at a small country temple, continued when he studied with a great Zen master at an ancient monastery, and then led him to Tokyo to get a master's degree in Buddhism. He had turning experiences and his teachers had pushed him to be free from these experiences. He had tried to learn to walk like a person of Handan and had forgotten his native way of walking.

After he told his boss in the bookstore, "Watching these books," he was immediately fired. He never held another job. In attempting to achieve continuity, he had indeed become a fool, an idiot, but the old boy had a long way to go before he could practice secretly.

7. Cleaning Under the Hedge

Once when Dainin-san was training under the guidance
of Daicho Roshi they were cleaning the grounds at Taizoin.
Daicho Roshi noticed that Dainin-san was not raking under
the hedge. He scolded the young monk, "What are you doing?
Look at the leaves under the hedge!"

"Nobody cleans under the hedge," Dainin-san said.

"Nobody cleans under the hedge," said Daicho Roshi.
"That's why a Zen monk cleans under the hedge."

WORKING IN THE TEMPLE YARD, a surprisingly surly Dainin-san appears with a defiant response to his old teacher's guidance. Where is this guy coming from?

Katagiri Roshi often said that Daicho Roshi didn't teach him anything, he just lived. Above we have a snippet from their life together. At about this same time, Dainin-san also went on a "monk strike." He refused to get up early in the morning for zazen. Daicho Roshi didn't say anything for a few days, then one morning he came to where Dainin-san slept and said quietly, "When it is time to get up, just get up."

Dainin-san obeyed and the strike was broken.

Also during this phase of training, Dainin-san asked Daicho Roshi if he could go and train with the famous teacher whom he attended at Eiheiji, Hashimoto Roshi. "You can go," Daicho Roshi said, "but you must know that a teacher can not change you. You must change you."

Dainin-san was deeply moved by this and stayed with his master.

For some practitioners, the purpose of training is to diligently polish the mind. Whenever thoughts arise, this perspective calls for us to bring the mind back to the still point. "Clarify, clarify, clarify," says one contemporary teacher.

For other practitioners, Zen practice is about seeing that there is not even a single thing. "Training monks sit in the hall and quietly observe emptiness," says Dogen. Only three of his monks, however, received his verification. Therefore, even sitting and practicing emptiness is not in itself worthy of obtaining the robe and bowl of authentic transmission.

Master Huangbo said, "The true Buddha is not a Buddha of stages." What goes beyond polishing the mind and quietly observing emptiness? What is true Buddha? How can we arrive at the spirit of a Zen practitioner?

If the true Buddha isn't a Buddha of stages, it isn't possible to add to or subtract from great emptiness, great perfection. And yet, this empty Buddha unfolds through time and space in wondrous patterns full of unique manifestation.

In what follows I present one way of looking at "Zen development." In my view, Zen development is not linear and neat but spiral-like and the stages are often not so distinct. Our first trips around the curves of the spiral tend to be aimed at "What can I get?" Many turns later, the spins may start to shift to "What can I give?" The separation between "practice" and "life" dissolves. The definition of the self may open up, collapse—and then reconstitute.

A robust sense of humor is important to appreciate the stages—and to laugh with ourselves.

The Zen development theory I offer follows these major stages: (1) Idealization, (2) Covert clinging to hopes for magical gain, (3) Extreme crabbiness at self and other, (4) Steadily walking without getting anywhere, (5) Experiencing fruition, (6) Falling into a well.

And then, of course, the spiral stages repeat.

People differ dramatically in how they move through the spiral. For some, development is gradual, smooth, and quiet like a teenager who gets only one small facial blemish during adolescence. For others, it is sudden, turbulent, and dramatic, like waking up one morning with a face full of zits.

What's more, in my experience, the people who become Zen teachers tend to be the latter type—we got noticed! Our development was/is often dramatic across the stages.

Also please remember that none of us are "done" going around through the spiral of Dharma. Tangen Harada Roshi said that his master, Daiun Harada Roshi (the root teacher of the Harada-Yasutani School), was still training and would be reborn again in Obama, Japan. And our earliest sources of the teachings of the Buddha show the Buddha practicing daily and going on retreat from time to time, still training—although not necessarily in order to get something.

Your teacher might have smoothed out through the course of training but unless she or he is a dead horse (in which case, my condolences) your teacher has rough edges and will continue to grow. Growth requires blunders. Your teacher might also dramatically fall into a well. This is not to excuse the teacher's falling into a well but to explain it. Many teachers in the past (and I too) have fallen into wells. If the past has any predictive value, many will fall in the future. Training rules and guidelines for ethical conduct may, at best, direct the fall into less disastrous wells.

NOW LET'S LOOK AT THE STAGES in some detail. In the first stage, *idealization,* Zen seems so cool, we love everybody in the community and the Zen teacher seems to possess something special, expressing what is in our hearts before we even know it ourselves. I might point out that while we are in this stage we are particularly nauseating for those that love us the most. We become "reborn" Zennists, spewing Buddha-talk that we are not living. The gap between our words and actions is vividly clear to those who really know our lives.

After a while the glamour wears off and the practitioner enters the *covert clinging to hopes for magical gain* stage. We begin to get more sophisticated and cover our original childlike and obvious hopes that somehow "Zen" is going to resolve our relationship issues, relieve our dysthymia without Prozac, and brighten our teeth. But the hopes continue. While quietly or even unconsciously attached to our utopian dreams, we construct a false, equanimous face with which we lounge around the dojo. Meanwhile, we have not really given up our magical thinking, believing, for example, that if we do Zen correctly we will be miraculously saved from our lives.

One of the unconscious forces that push the need to cover our true motivations is our shame that we in truth are amazingly self-centered. Ego wants to hide that little secret. In working with a teacher and a community, however, the gap between *idealization,* vowing to free all living beings, and the reality of ego manipulating spiritual practice for personal gain becomes increasingly difficult to smooth over.

50

Sooner or later, depending in part on how fully we throw ourselves into training, a perceived betrayal comes our way and the *very crabby* period begins. The trigger need not be dramatic. One friend simply saw his teacher slumping as he dragged himself up a flight of stairs after a long day. After a sesshin another practitioner discovered her teacher eating potato chips, drinking a beer, and watching TV.

From this point on the spiral, Zen utterly sucks, the community is a bunch of nut cases and the teacher is at best an ordinary person whose fault it is that our precious idealization has worn off—or that our stinky self-clinging has been exposed. Dainin-san seems to have been coming from this *very crabby* stage in his interaction with Daicho Roshi at the hedge.

At this stage, most people quit and go on to something else, imagining that the high of infatuation can be recaptured with another teacher, another tradition, or a softer or harder practice.

It is also possible that intensive Zen, whether monastic or lay, is just not what the universal doctor ordered for us. As a person who has stayed with the process, I can only speak from one side—from here it is clear that staying with Zen is *a* true path. However, it doesn't look like quitting is any easier. Once you stick your nose into Zen, you may find it sticks to you. Thus, it is rare to quit completely. Many quit only halfway, giving up on the inside but continuing to drag their corpse spirit through the appearance of training. Sometimes those who do quit completely, abandoning the forms of Zen, find it is stuck to their hearts and eyeballs, and there's no escape.

In any case, when a person decides that Zen isn't right for him or her, let's celebrate that clarity while not losing sight of the fact that it is right for someone else.

On the other hand, who's to know? Discriminating consciousness is fickle. How can we make this discernment? What once seemed off in my life, now seems like a perfect fit. Your teacher, despite his/her best intentions, may not be able to sort what is best for you from what is best for him/her and/or the institution's needs for you. Your friends in the spiritual community are also not reliable guides. They also have an investment in the outcome of your decision. In addition to wanting to avoid the loss of your sweet countenance, their secondary gain lies in having their choice to continue confirmed and supported by your choice. We are on our own here and as such this can be a wonderful opportunity to take full responsibility for our life.

IN MY PROCESS, one *very crabby* stage came to a head about the time that Katagiri Roshi decided to go to Japan on sabbatical in 1987. I had been trying for years to help create the conditions in which the Minnesota Zen community could work together more closely. It seemed to me that Roshi was like the hub of the wheel and we were spokes, spinning around him. Our connections to each other, however, were weak. I saw Roshi's upcoming absence as a great opportunity to address this situation. I developed a proposal to organize the thirty people in the core community into small work groups, each with a defined task—cooking, cleaning, teaching, ringing bells, and taking care of altars. These groups would get together regularly to talk about their lives and practice, in addition to taking care of their assigned Zen duty.

At a board meeting that August, I made my proposal. The members listened without response or rebuttal and then turned to Roshi. He cleared his throat, "Awww, when gone, anyway, I want Berk to take care of Zen Center as head priest."

I was hurt and furious. Had Roshi even heard me? It seemed to me that he was stuck in his hierarchical Japanese Zen model. I challenged him vigorously, arguing for "my" idea and enumerating the weaknesses in his plan.

Roshi sat patiently, eyes cast down. I had been learning in therapy about the importance of expressing anger and was internally very critical that Katagiri Roshi wasn't meeting my anger. He often said, "Fighting with me is like fighting with tofu."

After several minutes of passionate defense of my plan, feeling exhausted and embarrassed, I stopped. Roshi then calmly and deliberately repeated his plan. "When gone, I want Berk to be head priest."

Sliced through, the tofu's shape didn't change.

"That's it," I said as I stood and shoved back my chair, "I'm done with this ineffective, attached-to-ancient-Japanese nonsense."

I stormed out of the meeting, vowing to myself never return to Zen Center.

For the next several months I sat zazen on my own. This was a very quiet, balanced period in my spiritual life. To my surprise, absent community and teacher, I rediscovered my love for zazen. I frequently sat late into the night. I explored other forms of meditation, especially metta, loving-kindness practice, and delighted in the simple practices themselves. Also to my surprise, one morning about halfway through this period, I rose from zazen and began bowing, then chanted the *Heart Sutra*. The liturgy, which I had resisted for years, had become an important expression of my own emotion.

The activities of practice and life seemed complete in themselves. Somehow I had survived the *idealization, covert clinging to hopes for magical gain,* and *very crabby* stages—this time around (but, the path being a spiral, I could have known this stage would come around again). Nonetheless, a level field was opening up. This was *steadily walking without getting anywhere.* More subtle

53

work begins here. The practice at this stage is simply done for the sake of the practice itself. Searching for a motive at this stage is adding a head on top of a head. If we just stay with it, we might even start to get over our self a bit and direct our life to actualizing a purpose greater than ourself.

ONE COLD NOVEMBER MORNING as I was getting ready for work, the phone rang. I picked it up to hear my friend Ron's voice quivering, "Sarah died last night. Could you come over?"

Sarah and Ron contrasted each other more than any couple I knew. Sarah at forty-eight years old was a therapist, mother of two teenage boys, and a close student of Roshi. She was also interested in every New Age thing that happened by. Ron at thirty-two could have been the poster boy for the Red-Neck Revival Movement of Mid-America complete with a swagger, Southern drawl, and white T-shirt.

Stunned that Sarah was dead, I drove over to her house. Ron opened the door with teary eyes. "Come on in."

Sarah had a history of serious asthma attacks. She had such a severe attack one night at Hokyoji that two other Zen students and I rushed her to the nearest hospital in Waukon, Iowa—forty-five miles away. The student who sat with Sarah in the back seat and did CPR was also an emergency room doctor. She kept Sarah alive until we reached the hospital.

The previous night, Sarah and Ron had hugged good night and Ron had gone to his room in the basement. He had been downstairs only a moment when he heard Sarah rush down the stairs and burst into his room. She leapt onto his back and pulled his hair, desperate for air. Ron called the ambulance, gave her medication, and tried to administer CPR, but when the ambulance arrived seven minutes later, Sarah was already dead.

I heard this story as Ron and I drank tea. Nothing could be done or said. After about an hour there was a knock on the door. Ron looked at me sheepishly. "It's Katagiri. Didn't tell you he was coming 'cause I figured you'd leave."

I hadn't seen Roshi since storming out of the meeting in August. My breath tightened and blood drained from my face. I expected that he would be angry at me for having left Zen Center.

"Oh, Dosho-san, you are here!" he said, smiling and clapping his hands. "Good, good. We go now to the morgue for the after-death service. I need help. You come too."

Reality was completely reversed from my expectation. Together the three of us trudged off through the snow and cold. I drove Roshi's car as in days past. Ron sat silently in the back seat. At the morgue we were shown into a sterile room with stainless steel counters, white walls, and white sheets—so unlike the fertile field of Sarah's life. A bed with a body on it was rolled out to us. Roshi pulled back the sheet so that we could see Sarah's face. She looked tight and scared.

I served as the chant leader, intoning the title of the *Heart Sutra* and ringing a hand-held bell. Our mingled voices seemed to include even Sarah. I choked up as I chanted the dedication,

May the benefit of this penetrate into each thing and all places, so that we and every living being realize the Buddha Way together.

Roshi took out a *mala* and rubbed the beads together with both hands, simultaneously rubbing the rosary all over Sarah's body, mumbling the *Shosai Myokichijo Darani* in order to help Sarah avoid disaster.

Back in the car I asked Roshi about rubbing Sarah's body with the mala. "Doesn't believe she's dead yet," Roshi explained.

55

"Almost everybody's consciousness is very attached to body even after death. The sound of the mala makes consciousness pay better attention and realize that the body is dead."

Maybe Sarah realized she was dead. At the wake the next day she seemed relaxed and, indeed, very dead. Dead or alive, I was back together with Roshi. Performing the service together, I felt that our lives were entangled.

AS FOR THE NEXT STAGE, let me say it straight: *fruition* is fickle. Just when life starts to get settled, *fruition* might burst on the scene and upset everything, like receiving a bill for $5,328 on a credit card you thought was only in your ex-spouse's name.

Further, *fruition* seems to have a liking for odd places, a hospital morgue, for instance. And that's not all. *Fruition* will just not come in the form that we hoped. Throw your hoped-for fruition into the wind! That one will not come. We might want an insight that will be good for 200,000 miles but we get a lemon. Dogen Zenji tells us that we shouldn't necessarily even expect to be aware of our own enlightenment! That used to make me very, very crabby.

Most of us expect that with enough *fruition* our troubles will be over. Ah, sweet *idealization* (or sweet *covert clinging to hopes for magical gain,* depending on the volume of denial in the moment)!

In practice, *fruition* is more a trouble-maker than an answer to our prayers. Please hear this. If you are to continue and not become intoxicated by your insights, or at least not continue to drink quite so much, this is important. *Fruition* is a set-up for *falling into a well.* I'm not saying that you should avoid *fruition.* Please throw yourself into your life as if your hair were on fire. And know *fruition* is just part of the scenery of spiritual practice.

Remember that fruits become the object of awareness, like leaves under the hedge that we refuse to rake. We refuse to accept that the life we know through discriminating consciousness is already dead. Even death itself doesn't convince us. We've *fallen into a well,* know it or not. We're back at the first stage, albeit with a different vista, idealizing our life and not cleaning under the hedge, assuring the full employment of Buddha.

8. Does Zen Have Morals?

As a young monk at Taizoin (Peaceful Storehouse Temple) one of Dainin-san's duties was to prepare a bath for his master, Daicho (Great Tides) Roshi, by heating water with a small wooden stove under the bathtub. Dainin-san had to be careful with the fire so as to neither freeze nor boil the teacher. One day after Great Tides got into the tub, Dainin-san poked his head into the bathroom to see if the water was right. Without thinking, Dainin-san asked, "May I scrub your back?"

Daicho Roshi grunted, "No."

This offer and response were repeated during the next bath and the next. One day Dainin-san didn't ask. He directly entered the bathroom, took up the brush, and scrubbed his master's back. Daicho Roshi moaned, "Ahhhhh."

Afterward, Dainin-san asked Great Tides, "Why did you previously refuse my kindness when I asked you, 'Shall I wash your back?'"

Great Tides responded, "You fool! You are ridiculous! Don't insert any extra thought in dealing with something."

THIS STORY WAS A FAVORITE of Katagiri Roshi and his students. It is now used in some places to train teachers' attendants. However, the crucial matter enacted here is beyond the categories of teachers and attendants. How does it inform all of our lives?

Daicho Hayashi Roshi was a venerable old teacher with whom Dainin Katagiri Roshi trained in the late 1940s. They lived together in a small temple pressed up against a mountain, with a large rice field and small village between them and the Japan Sea. As the story indicates, Dainin-san was trained to serve his master.

He was also trained to serve the small village by keeping the temple schedule, weeding the cemetery, and performing memorial services. Clearly, a Zen monk is a servant. But who is service primarily for—the Buddha, the Dharma, or the Sangha?

A really old story explores this:

> Yunyan asked Baizhang, "Every day there is hard work to do. Who do you do it for, master?"
>
> Baizhang replied, "For the one who requires it."
>
> Yunyan replied, "Why don't you let her do it herself."
>
> Baizhang replied, "She has no tools."

Who is the one who has no tools? Who has no artifice, no contrivance, no capacity to hammer this, rake that, or scrub the master's back? In Mahayana art, she is sometimes depicted through blackness—unknowable to discriminating consciousness. On the altar here at Yugeji she appears as Prajnaparamita. During liturgy practice she does her very quiet part to intone the *Heart Sutra*. In zazen she manifests giving birth to Buddha and the community rises in turn, approaches the altar, pours tea over the baby Buddha's head, and scrubs her back.

Who is Baizhang serving? Sometimes there is no confusion and we can go straight ahead, following the letter of the precepts and the training rules of the environment in which we find ourselves. Sometimes, however, there is a fork in the road while trying to serve the truth. Stay or go in a marriage? What to say and what to withhold from a child or from a friend? Live this lie or that one?

For example, once while working in a program for adjudicated teens, I was confronted with a situation involving a young man who was HIV-positive. He wanted to go out with a young woman, also in the program, who was not aware of his condition. The young man told a coworker that he was not going to inform her of his HIV status because he was afraid that she would not go out with him. The young man also disclosed that he and the young woman planned to have sex on their first date. Worse yet, he shared that he would not use a condom. His privacy was protected by law and our boss informed us that we could take no action to help protect the young woman. As a servant of the truth in the situation we were in, what would you do? Abide by the law? Or would you violate the privacy of one person to protect another?

With their date night coming and without inserting extra thought into dealing with the situation, a coworker went to a pay phone and made an anonymous call to the young woman's parents.

What does the Zen tradition have to say to help us serve the truth? Are there any general guidelines to sort through ethical quandaries such as these? Given the ever-slippery ego, whatever guidelines could be put forward might well be co-opted to serve our self-first agendas.

Perhaps this is what Great Tides sensed from Dainin-san's offer to scrub his back—a false face, a manipulating ego, bent on easing Dainin's own anxiety. "Take that stinky thing outta here—I'm engaged in cleansing within and without" might have been the subtext to Great Tide's "No!"

Dainin-san came back repeatedly to investigate the obstruction. "May I scrub your back?"

He passed through by not asking. He served what the truth required by becoming a tool—a monk with scrub-brush in hand. To serve the truth could also appear as a parent with poopy diaper in hand or a youth worker with a pay phone in hand. But not here. Here it was a monk with a back scrubber.

Great Tides said, "Ahhhhh!"

KATAGIRI ROSHI taught that to practice Zen was to continually let go of the habit of satisfying individual desires and instead live in vow, serving our innermost request. The Great Vows are one way we express this in Zen:

Beings are numberless; I vow to free them.
Delusions are inexhaustible; I vow to end them.
Dharma gates are boundless; I vow to enter them.
The Buddha Way is unsurpassable; I vow to realize it.

Roshi called this "selfishlessness" And for this there can be no set recipe, no particular technique, just the willingness to be awake to everything, to investigate everything in the light of the precepts, continually drop our habit of struggling to satisfy individual desires.

This is our zazen. Whatever arises, Buddha's face or Mr. Potato Head, we throw all these heads away. Finally, no head remains. No mind, no heart, no body. Living in vow is simply the inconceivable and sometimes unbearable process of renunciation.

This is Zen talk—but is this really how Zen people live? Certainly not all of the time. We are all board-carrying-people (what the Japanese call "tanpankan," carrying a board on our shoulders such that we can only see in one direction) with places we cannot see, where we will not examine, where we will not even peek. "Know me by my delusions," writes Sallie Tisdale, ". . . We are sacks of karma. If I know your karma, I can know you."

Young Dainin-san showed his teacher one of his delusions. "Why did you previously refuse my kindness when I asked you, 'Shall I wash your back?'"

"You fool! You are ridiculous! Don't insert any extra thought in dealing with something."

Does this rough talk violate the precepts or training rules? Bahhh!

"Extra thought" refers to second *nen* and third *nen*. First *nen* is first thought or direct perception. Just living. Second *nen* is thoughts about first thoughts and third *nen* is thoughts about thoughts about thoughts. Second and third *nen* are not the enemy. Each thing has its function. They are, however, overused. As such, second and third *nen* are the ships we fools sail when we are fleeing direct experience. Flee or not, first *nen* is always as close as the water in the bath, the water that composes and sustains us.

Here is Katagiri Roshi amplifying this point:

Buddha says we should accept first thought, first feeling but don't be carried away by second, third, fourth. First thought can be accepted by anybody if you are a human being. Even though you see the shadow of death, don't be tossed away by second thought of death. Live fully now, that's all you can do.

This is Zen morality—bathing Great Tides. No one can avoid doing it. Yet most people give up. Without inserting any extra thought about extra thought, please, now, go on with your story.

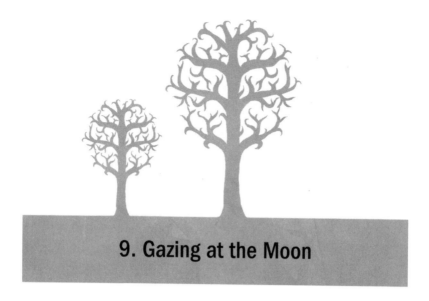

9. Gazing at the Moon

Gazing at the moon, Katagiri Roshi said, "Ahhhh!"

KATAGIRI ROSHI OFTEN EXCLAIMED, especially well into sesshin when the Dharma wheel spun most smoothly through his hands, "How sublime human life is!"

The "Ahhhh!" of Zen is not limited to the boon experiences, sometimes called "Big Mind" in some strands of contemporary Zen, that many students crave. Boon experiences are private mental incidents characterized by bliss, clarity, and non-conceptuality. They are like passing clouds and are neither samadhi (which is characterized by stability) nor realization (characterized by non-dual insight). Boon experiences do not reach the standard of the ancient way nor reveal the meaning of Katagiri Roshi's "Ahhh!" Throw them away as any deluded human sentiment.

A koan that appears in a collection called *Entangling Vines* (and elsewhere) vigorously highlights this point.

One evening Changsha Jingcen was enjoying the moon. Yangshan Huiji pointed to it and said, "Everyone without exception has that. They're just unable to use it."

Changsha replied, "Precisely. So let's see you use it."

Yangshan said, "You try using it!"

Thereupon Changsha gave Yangshan a kick and knocked him down. Getting up, Yangshan said, "Teacher, you're just like a tiger."

And we are the full moon. Ninth-century Changsha knew how to actualize the full moon as a tiger living in the mountains. Nineteenth-century Daiun Harada, while on begging rounds, saw steam rising from an old woman's urine at the roadside and was realized by this same full moon. But how can twenty-first-century human beings realize and make use of it?

IN THE SUMMER OF 1983, Katagiri Roshi, Tomoe-san, and three of Roshi's students, Ben, Meija (a married couple who were two of Roshi's priests), and I (before I was ordained), visited Japan to find a monastery where Roshi's American students might train in how the Soto tradition put "Ahhh!" to use. I was delighted to be allowed to go along as I was eager to get a taste of Japanese Zen and check out other Zen masters.

During the trip, we visited Taizoin, the small temple where Roshi had trained with Daicho Roshi. Katagiri Roshi had been appointed abbot of Taizoin when Daicho Roshi died some ten years earlier but hadn't lived there for more than twenty-five years. Although Katagiri Roshi wasn't interested in small-temple life, he felt guilty about leaving the villagers and not being present for Daicho Roshi's death. Not guilty enough to live there, however.

As we walked into the village from the bus stop on the main high-way, we were confronted with the vast expanse of the blue-green Japan Sea, complete with many dark green, cone-shaped islands, extending to the horizon on our left. On our right lay a strip of red-roofed houses, several blocks of brilliant green rice fields, and then Taizoin, sitting on the top of a slope that led to a small mountain.

From a distant perspective, Taizoin elicited a deep "Ahhhh!"—but close up it seemed small and shabby. Pictures inside showed an old thatched-roof temple that had looked even shabbier when Roshi had trained there. The floors did not feel safe to walk on as they moved in four directions with every step. The temple had been recently cleaned and was orderly.

Katagiri Roshi was received as the village's prodigal son, return-ing after years of absence. The villagers were delighted and attended to our needs splendidly. Each abbot has a benefactor fam-ily, a family whose primary responsibility is to look after the abbot's welfare. Roshi's family lived in a large, modern home. While the several generation family was engaged in preparing a meal, we waited in a traditional receiving room with aromatic new tatami mats, fresh rice-papered windows on sliding doors, and an alcove with flowers and samurai swords. Roshi took the swords off the alcove, stuck them in his belt and strutted around the room, occa-sionally announcing, "My family was samurai!" and pulling the sword out with mock threatening gestures.

During the next few days, Roshi would visit every family in the village for a brief service at the family altar, followed by conversa-tion, treats and tea, or sushi and sake.

WE BEGAN OUR FINAL NIGHT at Taizoin with a celebration with the (all male) temple elders. During the meal, Roshi told me later, the elders asked him to come back and live at Taizoin. They offered to rebuild the temple if he would return. Roshi gave them an evasive answer but he told me that he was thinking that he might move back to Taizoin to retire and train Westerners in Japan himself.

The women of the village created a feast of innumerable forms of seafood, most of which I had never seen before. Ben, a picky eater even in America, a regular meat-and-potatoes guy, had an internal list of a dozen acceptably edible items, and seafood—let alone small, dark, slimy creatures—was not on the list. In collusion with some of the temple elders, an alliance formed with winks and smiles, I helped convince Ben that the little critters were all forms of soy protein. Ben ate them reluctantly and reported liking one or two. When I confessed our ruse, everyone laughed and the difference between the Japanese and the Americans faded further from our minds.

Beer and sake flowed. Most of the Japanese men turned into radish heads from alcohol flush reaction. I felt at home. Somehow we found things to point to, make up some English/Japanese-ish expressions and laugh loudly.

A couple hours into the party I slipped out of the temple to use the outhouse. On the way, I was amazed to see an almost full moon hanging over the Japan Sea. As I stood in awe, I heard footsteps crossing the gravel temple driveway heading in my direction. I glanced back to see Roshi a few feet away, apparently also heading to the outhouse. I pointed at the moon. We stood together for several minutes enjoying the moon, then Roshi asked, "Outhouse?"

"You first," I said as I motioned for him to go by.

"No, no," he said as he leaned into me and put one arm around my waist. We stood again in silence. I was enjoying the moon and was so fulfilled to have this contact with Roshi but I also really needed to pee. At his lead, we opened our pants and peed together like two little boys on the playground, being bad.

As he peed, face to face with the moon, Roshi murmured, "Ahhh! Dosho-san. . . ."

The pilgrimage for me was complete. I'd come to Japan to experience Japanese Zen and to check out other Zen masters. I'd found a deeper certainty that I was with the right guy, Katagiri Roshi, that Zen is always this close—and is a real pisser.

10. Bowing Is Like a Rock in Your Heart

Katagiri Roshi said, "Bowing is like a rock in your heart. You cannot remove it."

I N 1977, after receiving zazen instruction, I started showing up for zazen and for Katagiri Roshi's talks. I immediately ran into a rock-hard barrier: bowing. It seemed that we bowed either standing or prostrating as often as bobbleheads. Enter the zendo, bow. Come to the cushion, bow toward the wall and toward the center of the room. When someone else came in and sat on either side, bow. Roshi enters the room, bow. To begin and end work, bow. Full bows were done during chanting services.

One morning during such a service a student stood at each of the ten seats in the Buddha Hall, a small room intended to be the dining room that we used for services. With the roll-down of a bell, we shifted to face the altar. With the last ring, hands palm-to-palm together in *gassho*, we bent our knees, quickly allowing them to touch the floor quietly, and then bent at the waist until our foreheads touched.

I had to dodge the rear of the person just in front of me to reach my goal. I placed my forearms on the floor with palms facing upward, and then lifted the palms and forearms as gracefully as I could to about ear height. To get up from the fully bowed position, I raised my torso upward and began shifting my weight onto the rolling balls of my feet. Just then the top of my head came into contact with something soft moving in my direction with considerable momentum—the butt of the person in front of me. I collapsed back to the mat and began again to rise with as much dignity as I could muster in the circumstance. Bowing practice was a Zen form of dodgeball.

What was all this bowing about?

I came to Zen because I thought Zen was free and irreverent, like Jack Kerouac driving drunk and frequently naked across America. Allen Ginsberg's *Howl* was one of my Bibles before I found Zen practice. I knew a large part of it by heart. Ginsberg knew the wretched aspect of life intimately: "I saw the best minds of my generation destroyed by madness, starving, hysterical naked. . . ."

Ginsberg also saw life's sacredness:

Holy! Holy! Holy! Holy! Holy! Holy! Holy! Holy! Holy!
Holy! Holy! Holy! Holy! Holy! Holy! Holy! / The world is
holy! The soul is holy! The skin is holy! / The nose is holy!
The tongue and cock and hand / and asshole holy!

For Ginsberg, everything was broken *and* holy. I resonated with this from head to toe. Wretchedness was all-pervasive. Holiness was all-pervasive. If so, why bow?

For Katagiri Roshi, bowing was an indispensable expression of Buddha, an essential motif in the "How to Practice" tunes that had been handed on from Dogen Zenji. "When bowing exists in the world," that old master had said, "the Buddhadharma exists in the world. When bowing disappears, the Buddhadharma perishes."

Dogen Zenji elaborates this point in his essay, "Negotiating the Way":

The endeavor to negotiate the Way, as I teach now, consists in discerning all things in view of enlightenment, and putting such a unitive awareness into practice in the midst of the revaluated world.

Training with Katagiri Roshi was an ongoing lesson in detail of how to put "such a unitive awareness into practice." His teaching was not so much about how to attain our original home as it was about how to make our everyday life the expression of enlightenment, unitive awareness.

Katagiri Roshi was determined to do what he could to transmit the Buddhadharma he had received to Americans. Bowing was a vital aspect of his conservative "body practice" and body practice was the field of play in which the true spirit of the Dharma was transmitted through master to disciple simply by the disciple following the body of the master.

For Roshi, authentically negotiating the Way with zazen and bow was nonnegotiable. When students questioned his conservative style of training, he remarked, "Even if Dogen Zenji came back to life and I was the first one fired, I would continue to teach just like this."

Roshi talked about bowing often, teaching bowing like a choreographer, both by words and by example.

Standing bow, gassho, was to be done like this: Palms together with fingers touching, thumbs touching the palm, tips of fingers at nose level, forearms roughly parallel to the floor but not so as to look like it was "Army training" (i.e., not militaristically stiff), bending from the waist but not too far.

Roshi modeled gassho beautifully with every entrance and exit from the zendo, with every opportunity. For him there was no "I'm-in-a-hurry-so-I'm-going-to-head-fake gassho." There were no dress rehearsals.

When giving instruction for full bows, Roshi taught us with a twinkle in his eyes to raise our hands gently because in this part of the bow we were uplifting the Buddha. "Do not flip hands up quickly or Buddha will fly over you," he joked.

IN OUR DIFFERENT WAYS all of us struggled to understand and actualize this simple practice. Later, I met a Japanese priest who had studied with one of the twentieth century's most famous and most severe Soto masters. I had heard stories about his teacher and was in awe of him. I asked wide-eyed, "What was it like studying with your master?"

"For twenty years I just arranged his slippers," he responded.

While I was struggling with bowing, this priest was arranging slippers, secretly practicing with the body like a fool. In either case, bowing or arranging slippers, Zen is not about being good or doing the moralistically right thing. Nor is it about currying favor with bowing or with a teacher in order to get recognition, ordination, or Dharma transmission. But that isn't to say that these things aren't entangled with the rock in the heart.

IN THE EARLY PHASE of my training, I kept mostly quiet about my resistance to bowing. I had heard from one of our senior students that someone at San Francisco Zen Center had once complained about bowing to their founding teacher and Suzuki Roshi had responded by modifying the beginning of morning service, adding six bows to the customary three so that the students would have more opportunities to understand bowing. Morning service at San Francisco Zen Center still begins with nine bows. I thought it better to avoid a repetition of that in Minnesota.

When I finally shared my brooding about bowing with Roshi he said,

> [A] bow is like a rock in your heart. You cannot remove it. From a completely different angle, you have to look at it. To practice gassho is to flow like water. When you gassho, just gassho. In the middle of "just gassho" there is no subject and no object.

I took Roshi's "rock in your heart" to refer to my resistance to bowing. Now I also think that "rock in your heart" refers to the fear of annihilation that is provoked by bowing, by embodying the dropping of self displayed when one becomes horizontal, one with the fundamental ground. Zen students must face the fear of annihilation or it may get acted out indirectly through anger at the teacher, avoidance of practice, swirling thinking in zazen, or by adopting a willy-nilly Zen philosophy that is disconnected from wholeheartedly saying "Good morning" to those we love.

Dogen Zenji seems to be addressing our fear of being obliterated by enlightenment in his "Genjo-koan":

> Our attainment of enlightenment is like the moon's reflection in the water. The moon does not get wet, the water is not fractured. Its light, vast and magnificent as it is, rests in a small puddle; likewise, the whole moon and the entire sky are reflected in a dewdrop on a blade of grass, as well as in a

single drop of water. Just as the moon does not break the water, enlightenment does not violate us; just as a dewdrop does not obstruct the moon in the sky, we do not obstruct enlightenment.

Reflecting on Dogen Zenji's teaching can educate consciousness and be solace at those times that we fear the moon. Making fear itself the practice through thorough intimacy with the bodily sensations of fear is actualizing the moon in a dewdrop.

As a young guy, I desperately yearned for the moon and got a bystander's high from the relaxed intimacy of Katagiri Roshi's words, presence, and especially his bow. Yet, persisting with the question of why we bow was something that I had to exhaust. And in order to persist, I found that I had to accept my ambivalence: lots of thinking and judgment about bowing (complete with old Tarzan movie flashbacks of "natives" bowing to the great white ape) *and* the aspiration to somehow personally taste the moon.

The more I chased the moon, the further I seemed to get from it. I was like a hound dog howling in the night.

Then during our monthly sesshin in January of 1980, I found myself intensely present for much of the afternoon. The muffled pounding of the bass from a stereo in the house next door stood out distinctly, illuminated by silence, blending with the smell of incense and the pain in my left knee. Self-talk was almost completely gone. Only an occasional "Gee, this is neat, you will certainly be enlightened soon" marked the open, intermingling field of the senses.

At the end of the sitting, we rose for service. Outside, a frozen Minnesota night was unfolding. Inside, the floor was cold to the touch of my bare feet. In the dimly lit zendo, nineteen students and Roshi began service. As I entered the first bow, my senses intensified to a body-shaking crescendo. Then "I" inexplicably dropped away and there was nothing. Rising from the bow, "I" returned to witness the mind reconfiguring the sense impressions into "things."

In returning to separation, I found myself really happy—and confused. Quiet filled even the nooks and crannies of the zendo. I was home and I didn't know how I got there. I wanted to bow to everything. Holy! Holy! Holy!

The chant leader began the recitation, "Maka Hannya Haramitta ShingyoOOOoOOO." And we joined in, "The Bodhisattva of Compassion, coursing deeply in wisdom beyond wisdom, saw all things as empty of inherent nature."

Of course! Bowing is also wide open!

I delighted in the sutra for the first time, tasting the message that compassion flows harmoniously with wisdom! Wisdom flows harmoniously with compassion! Tears of relief flowed. The sutra went on, "No eyes, no ears, no nose, no tongue, no body, no mind." No bowing either.

What had happened? The pivot of nothingness had spun me around. Separation plunged into no-separation and "I" disappeared for a moment. It *was* possible to do this practice like water flowing. It seemed in that moment that it was possible for "me" to do it. I swelled with confidence. I felt so separate.

PERSONAL EXPERIENCE had not removed the rock.

Can the rock be removed? One of the dozen or so stories Roshi repeated most often points to a door in the rock wall. A monk saw Huangbo bowing and challenged him saying, "You always say, 'Not seeking Buddha, not seeking Dharma, not seeking Sangha.' When you bow, what is it you're seeking?" Huangbo said, "Not seeking Buddha, not seeking Dharma, not seeking Sangha—one always bows in just this manner."

The doorless door arising spontaneously with bow is Huangbo's fully doing the practice *not* to get anything. Not to get merit from bows, not to get avoidance of the merit of bows, not to get special experience, not to avoid special experience. Huangbo's practice was just to fully embody this ineffable, ungraspable bow in its fullness.

This too is like a rock in our heart.

11. Not Using Zazen

*A student said, "Sometimes when I'm angry, I'll go and sit
zazen. It helps me calm down and process what I'm angry
about."*

*Katagiri Roshi looked down at the floor and grumbled,
"Don't use zazen in that way."*

THE STUDENT who used zazen to deal with anger, like many
Dharma students today, wanted a tool for his personal psychological process. This is counterfeit Zen. Although some good might
come from it, such a zazen is not the "wondrous way simply transmitted by buddha ancestors," as Dogen put it in "Negotiating the
Way." It is more likely ego seizing a new fascination, co-opting zazen
into a personalized system of self-grasping.

In 1988, in one of Katagiri Roshi's last Dharma talks, "Review
and Renew Buddhism for the Twenty-first Century," he made this
same point as if warning against what was to come in American
Dharma practice in the ensuing two decades:

As to renewing Buddhism, there is nothing to renew in Buddhism itself but instead *renew human beings who take care of Buddhism* [emphasis added]. Buddhism is mainly very conservative in order to maintain the essence of Buddha's teaching century after century. Wherever Buddhism has gone, Buddha ancestors have tried to maintain this essence. That is why Buddhism has flourished in China, Tibet, and Japan. If you forget the essence of Buddha's teaching Buddhism doesn't work for the long run.

Two points stand out here. First, Roshi suggests that rather than Americanizing Buddhism to fit practitioners (and increase membership in Dharma centers), we ought to maintain the essence and encourage practitioners to become new by fitting into the Dharma. From this perspective, it is not doing anyone a service to adapt the Dharma to make it easily digestible because it robs the practitioner of the opportunity to let go of the stinky, tired, old self and become new. Instead of rewiring our wacky heads, we want to rewire the Dharma to fit our wacky wiring!

The second point is suggested by Katagiri Roshi's phrase "renew human beings who take care of Buddhism." This is a different viewpoint on practice than the usual "what's-in-it-for-me?" attitude. Instead, Roshi viewed practitioners as people who were taking care of the essence of Buddhism in this time and place, protecting the fundamental so that those who come after us might have direct access to it. Currying favor with people by manipulating the Dharma and appealing to transient needs might very well result in blocking those who come after us from the essential point of the Buddhadharma.

Another characteristic of contemporary Buddhist practice, often encouraged by Dharma centers, is to combine meditation with other practices—community circles, twelve-step programs, psychotherapy, martial arts, shakuhachi, drawing, pilgrimages to holy sites, clowning, writing, yoga, cooking, and/or precepts as Moses' commandments. Whatever the teacher or influential community members happen to be interested in is combined with Buddhadharma and sold as the true way, perhaps augmenting the center's membership with people who aren't really interested in traditional dharma practice.

To visit some Dharma centers in America, take a tour on the web, or sightsee through the advertisements in *Tricycle* is a "Zen-and-the-art-of-motorcycle-maintenance strawberry-fields-forever" tour. I'm embarrassed to add that I'm as guilty as anyone, given the activities offered by the center I once ran.

Similar issues have faced previous generations of practitioners. What did Dogen do? In "Negotiating the Way," a questioner asked, "Will it be a problem if people who work diligently at this zazen also combine it with practicing mantra or shamata/vipassana?"

Dogen's reply:

When I was in China and had a chance to ask my teacher about the essence, he said he had never heard that the ancestors who properly transmitted the Buddha Seal from ancient to present times in India and China had ever combined practices like that. Truly, if you do not engage in one thing, you will never reach one wisdom.

Dale Wright, an important contemporary Buddhist scholar, takes this issue up in his *Philosophical Meditations on Zen Buddhism*. "Not all practices," he writes, "are equal in their qualitative powers." Wright cautions:

Although one goal in the Zen tradition is to eliminate the distinction between "ordinary" and "spiritual," this elimination is only effective when the ordinary has been elevated to the level of the spiritual, and not vice versa.

PICKING AND CHOOSING what we mix into our Dharma stew may simply be a way of co-opting Buddhism into our suffering worldview and may not lead to delicious freedom but to a tasteless gruel. On the other hand, inauthentic masquerading as pre-modern people and so rejecting the contributions of the modern world would also be false and also not free.

What's a person to do? In Dogen Zen, wholehearted zazen balanced with quiet Dharma reflection is the basis of true training. Other activities, like art practice, can complement and express our Zen or, like psychotherapy, can serve as a vital perspective on the ego, but lack the qualitative power, as Wright puts it, of zazen and Dharma introspection.

After all, wholeheartedly engaging upright sitting itself requires enormous devotion, as Dogen Zenji and virtually all the ancient and modern teachers report. Who really has the time to go deeply into more than a very few practices? Why then are practitioners in America often running around so frantically, sampling so many things? It looks like we have successfully integrated an American cultural element—multi-tasking! How can such dharmic multi-tasking really practice, manifest, realize, and attain the one wisdom?

Those in the past who have truly become people of the Way, women and men settled deeply in zazen-as-zazen, didn't use zazen as a tool for temporary psychological relief or combined zazen or (worse yet) Zen philosophy with other things in order to be popular or pay the mortgage.

By diluting the fundamental point and our lineage's unique approach, we betray our teachers and overlook the true jewel sewn in the hem of our robes. We might instead single-pointedly focus on this jewel. Only in so doing can we make a significant contribution to the blooming Dharma discourse in America.

In the Hayashi-Katagiri lineage, zazen itself is regarded as the primary expression of the fundamental. If zazen is not a means to an end (i.e., calming anger), what is it?

In an important talk, titled "Digesting Zazen Koan," Roshi noted:

I emphasize that zazen is a koan we have to digest in our whole life. Zazen is not the simple issue you have thought— a means to discover peace. When using zazen as a means you never have the great opportunity to digest zazen exactly in your life. Even though it is difficult, practice zazen in the appropriate way. That's why Dogen Zenji wrote ninety-five fascicles of *Shobogenzo,* explaining the meaning of zazen, the quality of zazen, the significance of zazen.

In order to digest zazen in our life, continue exploring the expression of the fundamental, and maybe glimpsing the jewel sewn in the hem of our robes, let's look at a passage from one of the source texts of Soto Zen, "The Thirty-Seven Conditions Contributing to Bodhisattva Practice." Dogen Zenji dynamically presents shikan-mindfulness:

Observing the body as not-pure means that one skin bag of the present observing body is the entire universe of the ten directions. This is the true body—a not-pure observing body which is vividly hopping along. No hopping along is no attainment of observation. No body is no attainment of practice, no attainment of teaching, and no attainment of observation. Yet the attainment of observation has already been actualized. You should realize that attainment is hopping alongness. This so-called attainment of observation is the daily activities of sweeping the grounds and washing the floor.

You didn't think the fundamental was going to be something that you could easily wrap your head around, did you? A passage like the above from Dogen Zenji could serve as Dharma food to sustain a lifetime of inquiry and practice.

Katagiri Roshi comments:

If you read this explanation of mindfulness in Japanese, it's like repeating a dharani. This passage of *Shobogenzo* is very difficult to understand because [Dogen Zenji] explains the whole of traditional Buddhist practice completely beyond the traditional understanding. If you understand it well, you will touch the deep source of Buddha's teaching, penetrating to everybody's life and all sentient beings.

Here's how I would express the Dogen passage: The insight body, the clear seeing body, is beyond the nets and cages of purity and impurity, peace or anger. This is the "not-pure" body. This clear seeing not-pure body of no fixed category is one stinking skin-bag and the limpid clear light of bliss. Still, it is simply the insight body—holy, profane, and undeniably galloping across the blue sky. In becoming one without intruding on the other, there is no rider, no horse, no movement, and no explanation. This wholehearted galloping of horse and rider is how attainment is actualized. We are already galloping the not-pure insight body. It is not found apart from rolling up our sleeves and going to work.

This is my present understanding and my present course of practice and teaching—not using zazen. Even if Katagiri Roshi came back and I was the first one fired, I would continue like this.

12. On Being Duped

A student challenged Katagiri Roshi saying, "We are often duped by devotion."

Katagiri Roshi responded, "You are too much involved in your individual world. Very much. Too much. Your understanding is not wide ranging. Not only you, if a person's understanding is very narrow, you are duped by whatever it is—Dharma, Christianity, or even the self."

WARM HUGS FROM DHARMA TEACHINGS may reinforce our way of suffering. In order to be free and fulfilled, most of us require teachings that sting. When the above student pulled the tiger's whiskers, Katagiri Roshi responded with strong words, meeting him with a verbal slap.

In contemplating this interaction, I'm reminded of a poem by Rumi, more popular for his words of love and ecstasy. Please reflect carefully on this in its wholeness:

The core of masculinity does not derive
from being male,
nor friendliness from those who console.
Your old grandmother says, "Maybe you shouldn't go to
school. You look a little pale."
Run when you hear that.
A father's stern slaps are better.
Your bodily soul wants comforting.
The severe father wants spiritual clarity.
He scolds but eventually
leads you into the open.
Pray for a tough instructor
to hear and act and stay within you.

Masculinity isn't dependent upon gender nor is the essence of friendliness based on consoling, writes the great Muslim mystic as if anticipating Jung. In my life, for example, my Polish grandmother was much more severe than my father or grandfather. After a couple glasses of her favorite celebratory beverage, Boone's Farm Red, she greeted every comment directed at her with, "Oh, piss up a rope!"

The feminine is equally important but when we want to go into the open *and* don't want to go, we need toughness. Still, sternness in the service of one's practice needs to be discerned from abuse.

In this regard, the following incident has been instructive for me. Once when I was attending a sesshin in a remote mountain monastery in Japan, I was particularly struck by the wholehearted-ness and playfulness of one of the monks whom I'll call Hodo. Others told me that he had been a police officer in Tokyo but suddenly quit and became a monk. Nobody knew what had happened that had provoked the change.

Hodo happened to be the abbot's attendant. At the beginning of devotional practice, the attendant's job is to be at the altar when the abbot arrives, offering incense exactly when the abbot is ready for it.

One morning, Hodo arrived at his place with the incense just a second late. The abbot immediately turned and punched him in the head hard enough to send a loud *THUNK* resounding through the Buddha Hall. And we were just about to devotedly offer sutras to the Buddhas! Hodo staggered back a few feet but held the incense upright, continuing to offer it to his master.

It isn't my business to condone the wanton hitting of monks. To the contrary, I've found in giving feedback to myself, Zen students, my children, and working with teenagers with serious behavior issues that a neutral tone usually works better than harshness or sweetness. However, it isn't the master's behavior here that interests me as much as Hodo's receiving the blow without flinching.

After the sesshin, I asked him about being hit. He didn't seem to be blaming himself or his master as he laughed and shrugged, as if to say like Tony Soprano, "Wha-chu you gonna do?" "Abuse" appears to be on the side of the recipient and Hodo showed no signs of being abused.

The important point here is how we receive the slaps of this life. "Don't bark first, don't bark back, don't bark at all," said Katagiri Roshi to dogs like us who howl at the first minor injury. A strong-spirited person, however, might bark back loudly as did a student some years ago when I struck her with the small kyosaku during a dokusan interaction. Without hesitation she swung back, hitting me in the chest at least as hard as I'd hit her on the shoulder. I was black-and-blue for days.

Depending on the circumstances, a teacher must respond as a living human being with access to many faces (happy, sad, angry, and all the rest) and resist the reifying and idealizing dynamics of community life that compel a teacher to become a dead archetype (always peaceful, tranquil, and unattached). Depending on the circumstances, it is important for a student to receive a slap from a teacher or from whomever it is that is delivering this moment's slap without wavering—or to swing back with penetrating clarity.

Now let's look at the content of the interaction at the beginning of this chapter. "We are often duped by devotion," said the student. In the Zen context, he seems to be referring to chanting sutras as we do several times each day during sesshin or in monastic living. In the West, this aspect of practice has come to be seen to parallel Christianity's devotional forms.

However, this projection does not fit. After first delivering his rebuke, Roshi went on to explain that what is often referred to in English as "devotion practice" is expressed in Japanese by *ki-e* or *ki-myo*. *Ki* is "to return." *E* means "something you can depend on." *Myo* is "the original ultimate state of life." *Ki-e*, Zen devotion, is to manifest returning to reality and gratefully sharing the benefits with buddhas, ancestors, and all beings. If a practitioner is actualizing *ki-e*, there would be no duping or being duped but unreserved expressing reality, including inexpressible gratitude for earth, water, air, and fire.

"You are too much involved in your individual world. Very much. Too much. Your understanding is not wide ranging. Not only you, if a person's understanding is very narrow, you are duped by whatever it is—Dharma, Christianity, or even the self," responded Katagiri Roshi.

"What do you mean," the student might have countered. "Doesn't Dogen Zenji say 'To study the Buddha Way is to study the self'?"

This is one of the most pervasive and pernicious sicknesses of Western Buddhism—using the Buddhadharma as a tool to enhance our obsession with the self. "But that's enough about *me*," quipped Bette Midler, "now let's talk about what *you* think about *me*."

90

We seem to forget that Dogen Zenji continued,

To study the self is to forget the self. To forget the self is to be actualized by myriad things. When actualized by myriad things, your body and mind as well as the bodies and minds of others drop away. No trace of enlightenment remains, and this no-trace continues endlessly.

Rather than misuse the Buddhadharma, grabbing a snake by its tail, what can we do? How can we forget the self endlessly? How can we cultivate wide-ranging understanding so as not to bite ourselves?

Simply put, "just learn the backward step, revolving the light around to illuminate." This is the practice of Soto Zen that Katagiri Roshi taught. "Revolving the light" is like the artistic method of relief: A mode of sculpture in which forms and figures are distinguished from a surrounding plane surface. Katagiri explained this metaphor like this:

If you want to carve a Buddha, usually we have an image fabricated by consciousness and we want to project it into wood. At that time, it's really a stinky Buddha statue. It is not alive, just a statue made by you who master technique. If you want to carve a Buddha in wood, the figure of Buddha should relieve space from wood, before you project your image of Buddha fabricated by consciousness. Buddha which has already been present in the wood appears.

Figure and ground are reversed, as if to say with old Master Mumon, "get upside down with this one." To sit like this is to attend to the ground as the figure, to sit in the wood as the Buddha already present, not something created by you, and relieve space. In this wholehearted zazen, the boundary between figure and ground, down and up, practice and enlightenment, particular and universal neither remains nor dissolves.

Katagiri Roshi said:

When we sit down in zazen, usually we think, "*I* am sitting." If we have a good zazen, then we think, "*I* have a good zazen." That zazen is *you* there. You and your zazen must relieve universal space. Zazen you do must be something more than zazen *you* do but zazen occupying the whole universe. At that time it is called *shikantaza,* Buddha's zazen. If you don't do this kind of zazen, no matter how long you do zazen you will never feel satisfied, you will never be free. Instead, you will be duped by a small view of Zen, deceived by a narrow view of life.

Therefore,

Everyday Zen Master Zuigan used to call to himself, "Oh, Master!" and would answer himself, "Yes?"

"Are you awake?" he would ask, and would answer, "Yes, I am."

"Never be deceived by others, any day, any time."

"No, I will not."

Zen Master Zuigan enters the play here calling to himself, "Master." As a matter of artistic relief, he might holler, "Hey, Ground!" and call back "Yes, Figure?" "Are you having fun yet?" "Yes, yes."

At such a time, the world of differences seems to be in harmony with the world of sameness, transforming through play that which is already fully alive and all-inclusive. This is the heart opening in a fundamental way, actualizing freedom and spiritual security.

Nevertheless, don't be duped!

13. Dainin's Four Essential Points

Katagiri Roshi taught four essential points for Soto Zen practice: (1) The oneness of practice and enlightenment, (2) that shikantaza is to bring wholehearted harmony to the self without attaching to enlightenment or delusion, (3) the Mahayana spirit to help others to live with others in peace and harmony, (4) finding life worth living under any circumstances.

ON SATURDAY, DECEMBER 20, 1980, Katagiri Roshi performed the home-leaving ceremony for the fourth time, ordaining a close student as a Zen priest. He read Dogen Zenji's "Words of Admiration for Home Leavers," shaved his student's head, gave her Buddha's robes, bowls, and the Sixteen Bodhisattva Precepts. Roshi offered these four essential points during a Dharma talk just a few days before in order to clarify priest practice, intimately addressing his student, those assembled on that winter day, and now you, dear reader. The private and the public intertwined, these four essential points Roshi saw as the call of the world, "This," Roshi said, "is the most important request [from the world] to everyone."

THE ONENESS OF PRACTICE AND ENLIGHTENMENT

This is an extraordinarily subtle teaching and is neither slump-and-slouch Zen nor hungry-ghost Zen. Underscoring the importance of practice-enlightenment in Dogen's Zen, Kaz Tanahashi writes, "Throughout his teaching career, Dogen hardly changed the tone of his voice. He simply expanded the variety of topics bearing on the same theme—practice-enlightenment."

Hee-Jin Kim sums up Dogen's Dharma inquiry like this:

How can practitioners authentically negotiate the Way in a specific daily situation, or in what Dogen calls "a Dharma situation"? This was the question Dogen pursued throughout his monastic life. . . . To put it in the simplest terms, it has to do with the manner and quality of negotiating the Way through dynamic, dialectical relationship of practice and enlightenment as two foci in the soteric context of realization.

Kim argues that the oneness of practice-enlightenment is not a merger in mystical union; nor complementary sides of the same reality; nor are they in the relationship of periphery and center; nor like the surface and core; not a transformation of one into the other; not like seed and fruit; not like cause and effect; not thinking and not-thinking; not worldly and ultimate truth; not antecedent and consequence; not means and end; and not nullification or denial of the differences between the two.

The oneness of practice and enlightenment is not "everything is Buddha, everything is practice." It is not "original enlightenment" as it is usually understood with the concomitant denial of the importance of karma, lack of concern for other's welfare, and enlightenment. Therefore Dogen Zenji cites the poem by the Zen master named Dragon Fang,

Those who in past lives were not enlightened,
Will now be enlightened.
In this life, save the body which is the fruit of many lives.
Before Buddhas were enlightened, they were the same as we.
Enlightened people of today are exactly as those of old.

Of all the not-relationships between practice and enlightenment, Katagiri Roshi stressed that practice is not a means to an enlightened end. If our practice is about greedily groping for spiritual experience, how could the result be anything but more greedy groping? War does not produce peace. Hatred of delusion does not produce love. Zen practice does not result in enlightenment.

From Katagiri Roshi's vantage point,

In the United States people use zazen in many ways. Even in Zen, zazen is still a means to an end, saying "You are Buddha but I don't think you are Buddha now so I think you should practice hard to attain enlightenment." At that time, zazen appears from a small territory fabricated by consciousness. It is like the stage of the puppet show. You are chasing after enlightenment, escaping from delusion, always chasing after. Wow! It is a part of the teaching but it is not exactly Buddha's teaching.

What represents the whole Buddha's teaching? In "Negotiating the Way" Dogen Zenji wrote:

A Zen teacher should advise his or her disciples not to seek enlightenment apart from practice, for practice itself is original enlightenment. Because it is already enlightenment of practice, there is no end to enlightenment; because it is already practice of enlightenment, there is no beginning to practice.

The meaning of "oneness" in the "oneness of practice-enlightenment" is the central issue here. Although practice and enlightenment are not different, they are not two.

It is like riding a bike on a trail. Is the bike the same as the trail? Obviously not. The bike is the bike and the trail is the trail. Is the bike different from the trail? Not so obviously not. In the specific Dharma situation of riding a bike on a trail, the trail causes, supports, and allows the bike to be biking. The bike causes, supports, and allows the trail to be trailing. Without the dynamic expression of bike and trail, neither comes to life as a vividly hopping along Dharma situation.

When we sit zazen according to the ancient way, we are like the bike and all the great enlightened sages are the trail. The practice of this moment depends on the great compassion of our predecessors in enlightenment. Bringing our predecessors to life depends on our getting on the zafu and bringing life to enlightenment. At that time, as Katagiri Roshi said:

The oneness of practice and enlightenment is to realize the source of existence that is filled with tranquility. At that time we appear in the vastness of the universe which is called Buddha.

WHOLEHEARTED HARMONY WITHOUT ENLIGHTENMENT OR DELUSION

Shikantaza has a specific form. The legs, either in a full- or half-lotus position (or as close as you can reasonably get), are like the roots of water lily, grounded in the earth, settled in the muck of this life. The spine is relaxed and straight like the stem of the lotus, supported by the water and inclining upward toward the sun, leaning neither forward nor backward, neither left nor right. The head, the flower of the water lily, sits softly on the top of the spine, eyes gazing downward at a forty-five-degree angle. The mouth is gently closed and the tongue rests on the roof, just touching the upper front teeth. The left hand rests in the right palm, thumb-tips lightly touching, forming an elliptic-shaped zero, expressing boundless openness.

In the assertive and increasingly subtle harmonizing of body, breath, and heart, a Buddha of formless form rattles our cages and shatters our walls.

Such a shikantaza is neither silent illumination nor cracking the head of a koan to find a kensho. This is the zazen marked by no fixed mark, the nonabiding Dharma with no fixed flavor—sweet, salty, or sour.

THE MAHAYANA SPIRIT

The Mahayana spirit is the great vehicle; carrying everyone across, no matter if you think we're already across or not. A Soto Zen priest's specialty, open to everyone, is bringing "already across" to life by putting others in our shoes.

In freeing others before ourselves we tend to want to be big shots, the one who saves others, many others, before ourselves. Katagiri Roshi once observed Hashimoto Roshi work with a communist-turned-Zen-monk on this point. Hashimoto-roshi would ask this monk every time he saw him, "Why did you become a monk?"

The monk would respond with the bodhisattva vow, "I want to carry all beings from the shore of suffering to the shore of Nirvana!"

Hashimoto Roshi would grunt and walk away. One day Hashimoto suddenly took a detour to the kitchen where the communist monk was working. He approached this monk from behind and when the monk turned around, Hashimoto Roshi grabbed him by his monk collar and shouted, "Why did you become a monk?"

"Roshi! I want to carry all beings from the shore of suffering to the shore of *Nirvana!*"

"Save yourself first!" shouted Hashimoto Roshi, who then turned and left the kitchen.

Hashimoto Roshi's Mahayana spirit, saving the monk before himself, is vividly clear here. Usually in Soto Zen training, though, the Mahayana spirit is manifested by quiet everyday behavior. Sitting zazen in support of everyone's freedom. Meeting someone in difficulty with a tender heart. Letting someone go first on the freeway. Forgiving those who we perceive as having done us wrong.

I don't believe that there are greater gifts that Soto Zen practitioners can offer the world in the Mahayana spirit beyond the gifts of practice-enlightenment and shikantaza. While the world is being consumed by means-ends dramas, a profound and penetrating vision like Dogen Zenji's, amplified by generations of clear teachers like Katagiri Roshi, and actualized now could help show that there is another way. Instead of the current "size" orientation in the Dharma world, focusing on the extent to which we've Americanized Buddhism as measured by the size of our budgets, the expanse of our meditation halls, or the size of our denomination, we could simply practice our religion, come what may.

FINDING LIFE WORTH LIVING

I visited Katagiri Roshi under difficult circumstances, bringing dinner for Tomoe-san, on the tenth evening of his hospitalization in January 1989. He had been in a near coma but his doctors had not yet found that he had cancer. As I entered the room Tomoe-san turned from her seat next to Roshi's bed with a bright and remarkably fresh smile. "Dosho-san, you are lucky. Roshi now is conscious for the first time."

Tomoe-san graciously received the food, said she would take a break, and slipped through the door. Roshi looked over from his bed. As I approached his bedside chair, Roshi gestured that *he* wanted to sit there. Not sure that it was okay with Tomoe-san or the doctors, I hesitated. Roshi was determined. I helped him into the seat and sat on his bed, directly in front of him. *What now?* I wondered.

After a minute, I asked naively, "How are you, Roshi?" No response.

Roshi sat with his back straight, hands folded together in his lap, eyes half open and cast down at a forty-five-degree angle. It took another long minute of staring at him to realize that he was doing what he did—zazen. I adjusted my posture to a more upright pose and sat with him.

Roshi gradually and gently slumped and his eyelids closed. After a moment, he startled awake and pulled himself upright, eyes cast downward and half open. He repeated this pattern numerous times over the next thirty minutes. Midway, tears started to wet my face and drip off my chin. I had never seen—nor have I seen since—such a resolute demonstration of intention. It seemed that the training had penetrated him so deeply that even when his body was too weak and his mind just barely across the threshold of consciousness, his vow was picking him up again and again.

Then I looked up and saw Roshi gazing at me. His expression was stern and despite his grey skin, his eyes were blazing directly and impersonally through me. "Roshi," I said, "it's Dosho."

His eyes softened and seemed to focus as they explored the figure facing him. He swayed slightly in his chair as if he'd had too much sake. He took a big inhalation, then said in a strong, measured way, "I know who you are."

How can I repay his compassionate presentation of practice-enlightenment, shikantaza, the Mahayana spirit, and how to make life worth living under whatever circumstances arise?

14. Throwing Open the Heart: How Do You Do It?

After a Dharma talk a student said, "The practice of emptiness is no emptiness."

Katagiri Roshi asked, "How do you do it?"

The student answered, "With emptiness we must be no emptiness."

Katagiri Roshi asked again, "Maybe so, that's why I ask, how do you do it?"

The student attempted to respond, "Well, um, sometimes it means. . . ."

Katagiri Roshi interrupted, "'How do you do it?' means 'How can you practice it?' Don't give an explanation; you have to do."

The student tried again, "You have to do without emptiness as a goal."

Katagiri Roshi raised his voice just slightly, "Still you are explaining. How do you do it?"

The student suddenly seemed to hear the question, "How!? How do I do it?"

Katagiri Roshi affirmed, "How do you do it?"

The student stammered, "Ah . . . um . . . just doing?"

Katagiri Roshi said, "Still you are explaining. The point is: how do you do it?"

The student paused, then laughed and said, "I don't know."

Immediately Katagiri Roshi said, "That's good."

SOTO ZEN IS ASTONISHINGLY PRACTICAL and the teachings, even the sublime meanderings of Dogen Zenji, insist on a whole-bodied response to this question: How do you do it? Chiming in from the grave, Chögyam Trungpa Rinpoche observed that Zen is "the biggest joke that has ever been played in the spiritual realm. But it is a practical joke, very practical." This is the spirit of action in Soto Zen.

Spirit is a word with many connotations. It comes from the Latin *spiritus*, literally "breath." Spirit is also a synonym for soul, "the animating or vital principle held to give life." However, no matter how long we look for that which gives life, or how to do it, we cannot find it. The eye cannot see itself—except by separation and reflection. Separation and reflection are bystanders in the Buddha world of doing it.

The above student is caught in a painful entanglement. He seems to have just one chopstick—thinking. What is the other chopstick? Katagiri Roshi said,

In the world of the Buddha we have to *do* something. We live in this world with the body and there must also be spirit. Spirit is heart, the source of existence. Manifest your spirit which is equal to the universe. The practice you do in zazen is exactly Buddha's practice, manifesting Buddha's world. At that time, the practice is something you do and it is spirit, the total manifestation of the universe.

Flailing around with one chopstick in the rice won't get the meal eaten. Just any *doing* won't do. In order for our doing to be in accord with universal life, the spirit must be dynamically alive—equal to the universe. Here "spirit" is the identity of our hearts with the perfectly tranquil and ungraspable source of existence. We are nothing but this. At such a time, the central issue in spiritual life shifts from getting an understanding (or a religious buzz) to action. How can we do it?

One of Dogen Zenji's ten cautions in "Points to Watch in Practicing the Way," is translated variously as "Immediately Hitting the Mark," "The Direct Realization of the Way," and "Settling Down Right Here." Such a range of translations might be due to the difficulty of the Japanese, *jikige joto*. The meaning is upside down from ordinary thinking. Katagiri Roshi explains,

> *Jikige* is "direct," no gap between. *Jo* of *joto* is to receive, absorb, or to assimilate. *To* is "it." "It" is the identity with the ultimate, exactly the fundamental itself. Together, *"joto"* means to assimilate, receive, and actualize it. We are it so we have to digest it and then we can actualize what we are. It does not come from outside. *Jikige joto* is direct assimilating and actualizing it.

When Roshi asks, "How do you do it?" "it" is the "it" of *to* that he is asking about. How do you do the fundamental itself, exactly with no gap? One level of assimilating this pickle is to understand the trap where the student is caught. He overvalues the power of understanding and talking. If Roshi had been Leonard Cohen, he might have sung, "I've been where you're hanging, I think I can see how you're pinned."

But Roshi was no sister of mercy. Instead of commiserating, he pushed the student's face right in it, asking the same question again and again, like that ancient master asking a monk, "Who is it that is worthy of the robe and bowl?" ninety-six times before the monk finally gave a suitable response on his ninety-seventh turn.

Being direct might take some time and patience! If so, it is time and virtue well spent. "Direct," *jikige,* is the fulcrum, the most important point of our practice. Katagiri has this to say about directness:

> "Direct" does not mean you get something directly, nor does it mean to try to know it. Instead, properly put your body and mind in the appropriate place. Then you are supported and *you are allowed to be realized* [emphasis added]. Instead of shutting yourself up in a small house—so called discriminating mind—throw open your heart.

What is the proper place to put the body? In Soto Zen we have many detailed practices, specifically manifesting how to sit, stand, walk, and lie down. To study Soto Zen is to study these four positions. And the spirit with which one takes them. Not only what to do but how. Finally, it is more a matter of what *not* to do, how not to obscure it, allowing ourselves to be realized. Throwing open the heart. Directly, immediately.

The spirit of directness is illuminated by Roshi's turning phrase, "you are allowed to be realized."

This is to reverse your everyday life where *I* always comes first. Then even if you go to the wilderness, *you* will not get the spirit of the wilderness. If you jump into the ocean, it is not that *you* try to swim. You are *allowed* to be swimmed by something more than you and your effort. The ocean, technique, teacher, your emotions, and many things allow you to swim.

When the pivot of nothingness spins us around, it is really a big shock—clear and complete from the beginning, majestic, pure, and seamlessly unfabricated—and not realized by chasing after things.

A story: Once there was a Zen master named Jimyo. His disciple was the director of the temple and every day he asked Jimyo, "What is the essence of Zen?"

Every day Jimyo said, "As director, there are many things that require your attention. Please go take care of temple affairs."

The monk became angry with Jimyo. He was already working hard every day so he didn't want to be told to take care of temple affairs. Meanwhile, every day Jimyo went to visit a woman who lived near the temple. One rainy day, the monk hid in the bushes and waited to ambush Jimyo. Just as Jimyo was about to pass, the monk jumped out in front of him. Without thinking and contrary to the monk's intention, immediately he bowed and stood silently. Jimyo asked him, "What are you doing on this narrow road?"

The monk grabbed Jimyo's collar and said, "Tell me the true meaning of Zen right now! If you don't, I'll knock you down."

Jimyo said, "You are the director of temple. Please take care of temple affairs."

Immediately, the monk knocked Jimyo down onto the muddy path. In that moment, the monk had realization.

Jimyo said, "If you hit the teacher, the other monks will accuse you of wrongdoing. You should not go back to the temple. You should go away."

Everyday, until this day, the monk missed the obvious. Everyday Jimyo had been calling, "How do you do it?" Everyday affairs are nothing other than eternity. When the monk was complaining, he was creating a gap between temple affairs and nirvana. Then Jimyo and the monk met on the narrow road. Finally, the master and the disciple became one. With the master soaking wet, the disciple melted into the master's life.

Jimyo's disciple had realization and then was sent away. He had become the teacher so could now go on alone, meeting it where ever he turned, allowed to be lived by the pebbles and the song of the cardinal.

The student in the story at the beginning of the chapter also did not give up but continued through at least six misses. Katagiri Roshi tried to narrow the road so they could meet, but just before a direct encounter, the student squeezed by. Roshi then affirmed the student's not-knowing. Roshi may have sensed that the day's work was done. With another student, he might have said, "It's not so easy, anyway," and continued asking, "How do you do it?" But here he simply said, "That's good," and let the matter rest. This might be fitting for a student so full of knowing. It may have taken ninety more "How can you do it?" for this fellow to allow himself to be lived.

Like it or not, our student did not have realization. A minute after Roshi's "That's good" he was back at it, analyzing, explaining, trying to look smart. The student was not yet ready to be turned, to allow himself to be lived.

Setting aside the student in this story, dear reader, after struggling for long, it may be time now for you to throw open the heart by immediately putting the body and mind in the proper pose, simultaneously manifesting how-to-do-it in complete unselfconsciousness.

15. Maybe Next Life

A student said, "Roshi, I've been thinking about rebirth for a long time and finally I've decided that I don't believe in it."

Katagiri Roshi responded gently, "That's okay. Maybe next life you will."

SCOTT, as I will call the student in this case, was a psychotherapist and an intense practitioner. He often drove three hundred miles to Minneapolis to practice under Katagiri Roshi's guidance. Scott's style was to examine the teaching carefully and forthrightly disclose his process. He often asked long and over-thought questions, fueled by large amounts of coffee and NoDoz, following Roshi's long and heart-filled Dharma talks as Roshi went beyond doing his utmost to help us understand the Buddhadharma.

After Roshi consoled Scott with, "That's okay, maybe next life you will," laughter erupted in our small zendo; the laughter might have broken the rafters. Katagiri Roshi joined in, getting the joke just a moment after everyone else. I happened to be closely watching

Roshi at that moment and saw his surprise when he discovered the humor in his remark. It seemed to me that his response had innocently come from wanting to encourage Scott and a deep belief in karma and rebirth.

Laughter and enlightenment depend on a deep belief in karma and rebirth. They are also fulcrums that will strongly impact the future of the Dharma in the West. Soto Zen has an important message, providing a non-humancentric, bias-destroying, inquiry-based alternative to seeing the world as the battleground of good and evil, right and wrong—if karma and rebirth are taught and practiced fittingly.

To the extent that we miss the dynamic truth pointed to by the vivid functioning of karma and rebirth, we may go the way of the Men's Movement—belching and farting our way into the *Catalog of Quaint Cultural Novelties.*

So: What is deep belief in karma and rebirth?

First this from Tibetan Buddhist practitioner and scholar Robert Thurman about denying karma and rebirth:

The seed of a little picture that someone holds, even subliminally, in their minds, planted by their materialistic education, that at death, Boom! Finished! That little seed, subliminally, erodes the sense of connectedness. It corresponds to an ingrained sense of disconnectedness and an atomistic individualism that has been cooked up over the last three centuries in the West.

From the perspective of disconnection, karma and rebirth are cultural trappings that can be cast aside in favor of scientific materialism. This perspective rests in part on a subtle form of racism—we Western white people know better than our little Asian forebears. Such practitioners misapprehend the teaching of nonself and find the teaching of karma and emptiness in conflict. At present, there are many who cherish this view. How sad that the path of the ancestors has become obscured.

Then there is another type who zealously accepts the teaching of karma and rebirth without reflection, without regard for modern developments in critical analysis, and without concern for the emerging context of contemporary global culture. Instead of acknowledging their own corruptibility, they use the precepts to judge others, and insert their own values and judgements into other's lives.

Such blind belief in karma and rebirth is a Zen version of oppression by the group, a modern form of power identified by French philosopher, Michel Foucault. Both belief in karma and rebirth and belief in no-karma and no-rebirth might be just head-trips. And those who believe in nothing are insufferable and said to be incurable.

Thus the Buddha warned:

Conjecture about the precise working out of the results of karma is an unconjecturable not to be conjectured about, because that would bring madness and vexation to anyone who conjectured about it.

Likewise, Charles Schulz wrote, "Sometimes I lie awake at night, and I ask, 'Where have I gone wrong?' Then a voice says to me, 'This is going to take more than one night.'" No matter how long we suffer and swirl trying to definitively understand our past mistakes and their effects on our lives and on the lives of those we love, we cannot precisely pin down many of the causes and conditions.

In order to avoid sleepless nights, madness, and vexation, the Zen school discovered a sideways approach to studying karma through wholehearted inquiry rather than circuitous conjecture.

We step away from obsessing about our own lives by quietly contemplating a story about all of our lives. Taken up sincerely, this meditation becomes an old-fashioned smack-down wrestling event with our self-clinging taking quite a beating. The story, known as the Wild Fox koan, was probably co-opted from folklore by spiritual geniuses. It goes like this:

> When Baizhang would give teachings to the assembly an old man would often appear and listen to his Dharma talks. The old man usually left after the talks, but one day he remained behind. Baizhang asked, "Who are you?" The old man said, "I am not actually a human being. In ancient times, at the time of Kashyapa Buddha, I lived and taught on this mountain. One day a student asked, 'Does a person who has cultivated great practice still fall into cause and effect?' I said to him, 'No, such a person does not.' Because of this I was reborn as a wild fox for five hundred lifetimes. Venerable Master, please say a turning word and free me from this body of a wild fox." Then he asked Baizhang, "Does a person who has cultivated great practice still fall into cause and effect?" Baizhang said, "Do not ignore cause and effect." Immediately the old man had a great realization.

Like karma and rebirth, the koan is complex, subtle, and shapeshifting, some days appearing with many layers and pungent like an onion, and some days appearing with many layers and sweet like parfait. The Wild Fox koan invites quiet sitting and deep reflection again and again over many years, life after life.

Even the design of the story contains a critical message. The meeting between Zen master Baizhang and the old man begins in community but culminates in a dyad, in the play of one and two.

This play is essential because ego cannot see itself and therefore we cannot truly train alone. For example, if we were to hang out in our own basement, kicking and punching the air in a self-styled manner, our friends would laugh at us if we said we were training in Shotokan Karate. Hanging out alone and sitting zazen without having fully integrated and gone beyond the guidance of a teacher is likewise not Zen and we will be laughed at even by the spiders and cuddle bugs.

Instead of practicing alone, we might rely on practice with a group, over-valuing the opinions of those who themselves have not plumbed the depths or at least gotten their midriffs wet. Most likely such a practice will also not be so deep. A key passage for Dogen Zenji from the *Lotus Sutra* explicates this point:

Only a buddha together with a buddha can fathom the Reality of All Existence, that is to say, all existence [has] such a form, such a nature, such an embodiment, such a potency, such a function, such a primary cause, such a secondary cause, such an effect, such a recompense, and such a complete fundamental whole.

Only a buddha together with a buddha—Dogen's Zen arises from this point, not from the modern preference that the community can function as buddha. After all, it is difficult enough to meet one person face to face, buddha together with a buddha, let alone meet dozens of people squirming on their zafus.

Once the community leaves, Baizhang's deep-belief-in-karma inquiry begins, "Who are you?" We learn that the present old man was once the abbot of Baizhang Mountain. In the ancient Zen custom the master and mountain were not regarded as two things. The abbot wore the name and became the mouth-piece for the mountain.

Therefore, the present old man would also have been named Baizhang in the timeless past. When the present Baizhang faced the former Baizhang, he faced himself; he looked into the face of the cause of which he is the effect. Here Baizhang presents a moving model for dealing with our own pasts—looking it straight in the eye and asking, "Who are you?"

Karma and rebirth appear to have been thoroughly embraced by both the old-time Wild Fox storytellers and their audiences. The teaching of karma, the story behind the story, says that bright actions lead to wholesome results. Dark actions lead to unwholesome results. Actions mixed with both bright and dark intentions, characterizing most of human behavior, have mixed results. However, when we are hurt, angry, or fearful, we tend to see others' motivations as entirely bright or dark, forgetting or blinding ourselves to our own propensity for action coming from mixed intentions, forgetting to use the precepts as a mirror rather than a weapon.

Realizing the true nature of the swirl of bright, dark, and mixed is enlightenment. Enlightenment, according to the original Buddha's teaching, is the end of suffering for the individual. Originally, the teaching of karma and rebirth functioned in Buddhist societies to assure the faithful that, despite the seeming empirical evidence in their faces (dark actions that led to fame and wealth and bright actions that led to sickness and poverty), sooner or later the law of the just universe would get things right.

The Judeo-Christian tradition addresses the issue of justice and injustice through the Book of Job. Late in the story, Job's loved ones have been killed, his property has been taken, and his body is covered with oozing boils as a result of a plot wherein God and Satan were co-conspirators. The ever-righteous Job finally questions God and God responds out of the whirlwind,

Who is this that obscures divine plans with words of
ignorance?
Gird up your loins now, like a man;
I will question you, and you tell me the answers!
Where were you when I founded the earth?
Tell me if you have understanding. . . .
And who shut within doors the sea,
when it burst forth from the womb;
When I made the clouds its garment
And thick darkness its swaddling bands?

In other words, it isn't proper for even pious large-brained pri-
mates to question the omniscient. And yet every Zen student worth
his or her salt has the strength and the will to question fixedly.

If you haven't read the Book of Job recently, you might review it
through "The Goon Bible Project—Book of Job" on YouTube. In
just under four minutes you can see a blistering version of the story,
including God and the Devil enjoying a conversation with martinis,
apparently a respite to Satan's walking to and fro upon the earth,
and planning how to mess with God's most blameless servant.

The Mahayana's broken-hearted compassion arises from sitting
in the ashes next to Job. The heart's innermost request, humanity's
greatest love to free all beings, not limiting ourselves to simply puri-
fying our own karma, ending our own suffering, and escaping from
future rebirths, explodes the scope of enlightening action from this
point and turns us to embrace the other as ourselves—humans, wild
foxes, and the unknown. Karma and rebirth become the field of
play for enlightening beings who invite rebirth—life after life—in
order to suffer together and free everybody.

The Wild Fox koan contributes to the conversation by responding to original Buddhism's emphasis on individual salvation and to

the Mahayana's cry to hear the suffering of all beings by insisting on a response from the thick of suffering, just and unjust. The Wild Fox koan is as raw and revolutionary as the story of Job that Jung believed demanded the answer of Christ, a reply to God's brutal exploitation of human decency.

Likewise, the wild fox barks until we respond in kind.

Our former Baizhang, the present old man, responded. He answered the question properly according to original Buddhist group norms and was launched into five hundred lives as a wild fox—a tricky shapeshifter whose bark was worse than his bite. This sounds a lot like Ego.

Here a person of great practice, a person who had not only perfected bright actions and their wholesome effects but had also penetrated to the core of the universal mystery, became a fox and a wild one at that. Perhaps rebirth as a wild fox arose due to the former Baizhang's overstatement of the case, his focus on individual liberation, and attachment to attainment.

If asked today, "Is a person of great practice free from karma?" I would respond, "What about the tide that lifts all boats?"

There was a time in my life, in what now seems like a lifetime ago, intoxicated by the intensity of Zen training, when I acted as if I were free from karma. I believed that I and others would not reap the effects of my actions. I lost my humanity for a while and became like a wild fox. The belief that a person of great practice, great enlightenment, is free from cause and effect might lead half-baked potatoes like me, driving under the influence of Zen, to commit harmful actions. For others, the belief that some special person is free might also lead to seeing no evil until after an explosion of repressed observations. Then such a person might see only evil.

Short of any acting out, in the Wild Fox koan the correct answer seems to have been enough to result in reinforcing ego, like Bill

Murray's character in the movie *Groundhog Day* who returns repeatedly, for perhaps 500 lives, to the same day in Punxsutawney, Pennsylvania, until he can serve and love skillfully.

Or perhaps the correct answer simply isn't always correct. In what circumstances would "An enlightened person does not fall into cause and effect" lead to freedom for the monk and for every bystander?

Further, you have to wonder, who is this old man? Whatever became of a just universe? What about "not falling" led to five hundred lives as a wild fox and what about "not ignoring" led to great enlightenment? Do "turning words" really have the power to turn the heart? Is the call of the insentient (e.g., the sound of the wind in the cotton wood tree) different from the "turning word" of the koan? What became of the wild fox after his enlightenment? Finally, if the world isn't the battleground of good and evil unless we make it so, how shall we live today?

The Wild Fox koan is a call of the wild, beckoning us to broaden the limits of our capacity to allow for open-ended possibilities. When we grope for a fixed idea about any of the above questions, or about the precise effects of our own past karma, we meet manifold double-binds and are caught in sleeplessness, madness, and vexation brought on by conjecture about what is not to be conjectured about by one who is not interested in chasing his or her tail.

The koan leaves no other way through than to relax into the periphery along the hedge row where the scent of the wild fox, the scent of the subtle meaning of karma and rebirth, diffuses harmoniously with this very birth and death.

When we come to this point, panting, desperate, and ready for a new approach, poet W.S. Merwin might provide direction. His poem "Fox Sleep" begins with this reflection of the Wild Fox koan:

On a road through the mountains with a friend many years ago / I came to a curve on a slope where a clear stream / flowed down flashing across dark rocks through its own / echoes that could neither be caught nor forgotten. . . .

The friend here could be Scott or Katagiri Roshi. It might be an old man, a wild fox, or our own reflection in another's eyes. The slope is curved—easy to slip and fall in love—yet the water must be clear for the reflection of the flashing flow to be just the reflection of the flashing flow. The echoes echo echoes. And sometimes when we get to thinking of the past, we find that we can neither get hold of it nor let go of it. We must stop like a watcher who waits for the dawn until the day when all the others leave. Then in the swirl of our past, present, and future, in the tangle of repetition and freedom, we might meet face to face.

At just such a time, how will we be reborn?

16. Hair on Fire

At a sparsely attended introductory session led by Katagiri Roshi, person after person asked about the physical pain of zazen. Roshi took some time to arrange himself, adjusting his robes and his sitting cushion. Finally, he cleared his throat and stared at the floor a few feet in front of his cushion. Then Roshi said, "You won't know how much pain you're in until you are enlightened."

HERE GREAT PATIENCE ROSHI fully disclosed his red heart. His statement put an end to the questions about pain and none of those present returned to Zen Center—only an old Dharma friend auditing the session lived to tell this story. Who wants to hear that rather than a blissful otherworldliness, enlightenment is to know suffering all the way through?

There may be a few but not many. News has reached here that one senior Western teacher kept track of the number of students that came through his door and concluded that about one person in five thousand stayed and trained for ten years.

Of the many barriers to ten years of practice, the first barrier is pain. According the Katagiri Roshi, enlightenment is also about pain. The Soto Zen way of practice-enlightenment certainly includes pain, but does it also include freedom from suffering?

Unlike the situation in the above incident where a small group attended an introductory session, at my introduction to Zen with Katagiri Roshi, I was the only student. Roshi ushered me into a small room and we sat face-to-face a few feet apart. He then simply and joyfully did what he was there to do. "There are three aspects of zazen," Roshi began, "which really aren't three things: body, breath, and mind."

Away Roshi went as if he were speaking to a group of thirty instead of just one young, ragged hippie wanna-be in tight, holey blue jeans. My body was not well suited to sitting on a cushion on the floor for more than five minutes. After ten minutes, both legs were dead asleep. Katagiri Roshi said not to worry about sleepy legs. "Your legs also need a nap sometimes."

After fifteen minutes my legs woke up with the most intense, throbbing knees (and then too often for the next ten years, I was in physical, emotional, and/or existential agony during zazen, especially during sesshin). Roshi didn't seem to mind that I was in pain:

In zazen, the body is upright, like a Bodhidharma doll. You know the Bodhidharma doll? Bodhidharma doll is like this [then he hit himself sharply in the chest, rolled way back on his cushion and sprang back up, laughing]. Zen monk sits so that whatever comes up, he bounces back, just like doll. Even if you hit the floor, you bounce back. Seven times down, eight times up. Whatever happens, you spring back. Do you understand? Anyway, someday maybe you will understand.

Seven times down, eight times up—one more time up than down, so we must start on the floor, probably face down in dookie.

That session with Roshi was thirty hitting-the-floor years ago. Writing about my old master now, my heart laments. He was extraordinarily kind to me. "You will have lots of spiritual experiences but they are just scenery," he told me in our first meeting. "You must be long-distance train, anyway. Do you understand? Long-distance train. Most important point is to reach final goal."

I regret to report that in the face of his kindness, I was habitually ungrateful. The thirteen years of training with him were so fleeting and I missed so many opportunities to repay my debt for his compassion! All the more to digest in the past eighteen years (and the next eighteen, I pray).

In order to repay this debt, or at least make a payment on my installment plan, here is a quick course in Zen—the entangling of our predicament, the barriers, and the solution.

For starters, everybody knows that time flies, but who faces the truth of this rapidly flying by life-and-death?

"Time is pilin' up, we struggle and we scrape / We're all boxed in, nowhere to escape." So sings Bob Dylan.

Recognizing our desperate situation is the crossroad of art and spirituality. To train, not just sing and dance about our predicament, is to directly face life and death. This is the manifestation of true Zen. We can tell ourselves stories about not fearing death or distract ourselves with relationships, media, jobs, or practices that make us feel good, but when we die we'll still piss and shit ourselves. With our days numbered, we struggle, scrape, and play people games to avoid the brutal truth of being trapped.

As William Shakespeare wrote in *Macbeth*:

All my pretty ones?
Did you say all? O hell-kite! All?
What, all my pretty chickens and their dam
At one fell swoop?

"Fearing the swift passage of the sunlight," Dogen Zenji might have said to wily William, "practice the Way as though saving your head from fire."

How would you practice if your head were on fire? Even Shakespeare, with all his soaring through the verbal human world, would act with wild abandon and with no extra concerns. I doubt anyone with their hair on fire would over-think the situation, "I'll pat it out gradually so as not to burn my hands." Or wallow in self-clinging, "I'll do it when I'm good and ready." Or place sundials in the shade, "I'll just breathe, smile, and be peace." Or get oppositional, "I won't do it at all because I hate doing what I'm told."

We might build a universe-illuminating fire with all the pabulum spewed out justifying self-clinging just in this generation. Even contemporary Dharma teaching mostly encourages easygoing practice, grooming the leaves rather than cutting the root. "Why level downward to our dullest perception always," I wonder with Thoreau, "and praise that as common sense? The commonest sense is the sense of men asleep, which they express by snoring."

An easy-going attitude, willy-nilly Zen, has real life consequences. Several years ago, for example, I met from time to time with a student who reported being very stuck in his practice. Like most people, he seemed to be thinking his Zen and expected unexcelled, complete, perfect enlightenment while practicing halfheartedly, spinning in his old grooves. The student had not yet chosen a teacher and was occasionally meeting with me and sometimes someone else. One day, the other teacher asked me what suggestions I had for this student. "I encourage him to practice wholeheartedly as if his hair were on fire," I reported.

"Really?" she said sounding quite surprised, "I tell everybody to take it easy."

Those who attended Roshi's introductory session understandably didn't want to face pain and maybe they were looking for an easy-going way—or at least support from a teacher in their stuckness. In such situations, so-called teachers perform a heartrending disservice by coddling would-be students, literally selling a bill of goods rather than the beyond-sale good itself. Many of us in American Dharma circles act in such a manner, stricken with what Ken Wilbur calls Boomeritis.

In American Soto Zen, the symptoms of Boomeritis often appear as attachment to psychological healing and confusion about the meaning of "no attainment." If the disease proves more potent that the medicine, Boomeritis Zen will likely spread to the next generation, if there is a next generation. If the authentically transmitted eye of Dharma were as it appears from diseased vision, the Buddhas would never have appeared in the world nor could the Buddhadharma have survived until today.

The poet-monk Ikkyu provides an inspiring touchstone for practice. He wrote:

sick of it whatever it's called sick of the names
I dedicate every pore to what's here

Old Ikkyu knew wholehearted zazen. He also wrote:

raging in the now hungry for it
crows rattle the air no dust

When we throw ourselves into zazen, into this very life, we enter the gate of joyful ease and the Way is complete in all the ten directions. *Right here* is the truth-happening place, and the shoes that are already on our feet fit so nicely. At such a time, enlightenment is fully intimate with suffering. This or that pain or complaint co-create this moment along with the rattle of the far-off crow.

The second most important thing, friend, is not to worry about *you*. Don't worry about you if you are just taking up Zen or if you have practiced wholeheartedly for many long years, through many long retreats, with or without the results you desire. Forget attainment or nonattainment and just burn completely in zazen and in each activity day and night.

The most important thing is the strength of the Way-Seeking Heart.

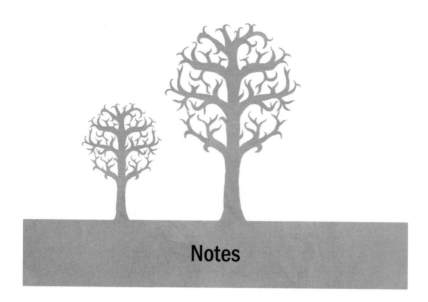

Notes

INTRODUCTION

The full story of the Buddha and Vakkali can be found in Bhikku Bodhi's translation of *The Connected Discourses of the Buddha,* pages 938–41.

CHAPTER 1: NOT GETTING ZEN

The story that begins the chapter was found in an interview with Socho Koshin Ogui in *Tricycle,* Summer 2006.

The dialogue between the members of the P'ang family is based on a translation in *A Man of Zen: The Recorded Sayings of Layman P'ang,* by Ruth Fuller Sasaki, Yoshitaka Iriya, and Dana Fraser. Zen stories are most often about monks. Layman P'ang and his family represent a refreshing alternative ideal image of training. I've made some minor changes in wording of the story.

The story about an interaction with Katagiri Roshi about desire utilizes the version of the Great Vows chanted at the Minnesota Zen Center when I studied with Katagiri Roshi. The *Soto School Scriptures for Daily Services and Practice,* an important collaboration between scholars and American Soto Zen teachers, sponsored by Japanese Soto Zen has "Delusions are inexhaustible; I vow to end them."

The six perfections or *paramitas,* essential practices in Mahayana Buddhism, include giving, morality, patience, effort, concentration, and wisdom. More about the paramitas can be found in *The Practice of Perfection: The Paramitas from a Zen Buddhist Perspective,* by Robert Aitken.

Dogen Zenji's comments on giving can be found in "Bodhisattva's Four Methods of Guidance," in *Moon in a Dewdrop: Writings of Zen Master Dogen,* edited by Kazuaki Tanahashi. The other three methods are kind words, beneficial actions, and identification (putting others in our shoes). The study of Dogen's writings are an important aspect of Katagiri Roshi's Zen and "Bodhisattva's Four Methods of Guidance" is especially accessible and was written, it seems to me, with lay practitioners in mind. Katagiri Roshi's comments to "Bodhisattva's Four Methods of Guidance" can be found in *Returning to Silence: Zen Practice in Daily Life.*

The translation of the passage from "Universally Recommended Instructions for Zazen" comes from the *Soto School Scriptures for Daily Services and Practice.*

CHAPTER 2: JUST A QUESTION ABOUT TECHNIQUE

I discovered the interaction that begins this story on a CD, "Mindfulness," March 23, 1984, by Katagiri Roshi, issued by the Minnesota Zen Meditation Center. I can hear my voice in the chanting that begins and ends the talk but have no memory of this interaction! All of the Katagiri Roshi CDs cited here are available from the Minnesota Zen Center. I am indebted to them for their careful work, preserving Katagiri Roshi's talks in order to provoke this student's memory concerning what he taught.

Steven Heine's book, *Zen Skin, Zen Marrow: Will the Real Zen Buddhism Please Stand Up?*, also contains an important discussion of Zen precept practice in the epilogue, "The Real Zen Buddhism: Engaged, Enraged, or Disengaged." Steven Heine, along with William Bodiford, Dale Wright, and others, represents a new generation of Western Buddhist scholars whose practitioner-oriented research is both challenging and illuminating.

CHAPTER 3: THE DYNAMIC WORKING OF REALIZATION

For more on "The Meaning of Practice and Verification" (*"Shushogi"*), see *Buddhism in the Modern World,* edited by Steven Heine and Charles Prebish, Chapter 7: "Abbreviation or Aberration: The Role of Shushogi in Modern Soto Zen Buddhism" by Steven Heine.

CHAPTER 4: WE DON'T STUDY KOANS

Recent research casts considerable doubt on the Soto Zen sect's religious history in regard to the role and function of koans in Soto Zen and many other topics. See Steven Heine's *Dogen and the Koan Tradition: A Tale of Two Shobogenzo Texts* and Steven Heine and Dale S. Wright's *The Koan: Texts and Contexts in Zen Buddhism.*

For an example of pithy koan commentary by medieval Japanese Soto monks, see *The Iron Flute: 100 Zen Koans* by Nyogen Senzaki and Ruth Strout McCandless.

The passage from Dogen's "Great Practice" (*"Daishugyo"*) in this chapter is from an unpublished translation by Kazaki Tanahashi and Dojun Dan Welch.

For much more on shikantaza, see *The Art of Just Sitting: Essential Writings on the Zen Practice of Shikantaza,* edited by John Daido Loori.

For koan practice, *Sitting with Koans: Essential Writings on the Practice of Zen Koan Introspection,* also by John Daido Loori (with Tom Kirchner) is excellent. There are many commentaries specifically on muji available in English. See *Zen Comments on the Mumonkan* by Zenkei Shibayama for one contemporary Japanese view and *Bring Me the Rhinoceros and Other Zen Koans to Bring You Joy* by John Tarrant for a contemporary Western view. Tarrant's chapter title "Zhaozhou's Dog: The Secret Changing of Your Heart" suggests the boundless variety in which mu can present and the delightful play of Tarrant's style.

For a creative modern integration of Dogen and koan Zen, see John Daido Loori and Kazuaki Tanahashi's *The True Dharma Eye: Zen Master Dogen's Three Hundred Koans.*

CHAPTER 5: ALREADY YOU ARE STUCK

The quote from Hashimoto Roshi is from his commentary on Dogen's "Bodhi Mind" chapter of the *Shobogenzo,* based on an unpublished translation work-in-progress by Kenneth Port and the author.

The questions from Dogen's commentary on the Wild Fox koan come from "Great Practice" *("Daishugyo")* in *Master Dogen's Shobogenzo: Book 4,* translated by Gudo Nishijima and Chodo Cross, 47.

CHAPTER 6: CLAY BALLS AS TOILET PAPER

This story, "How stupid you are," comes from my memory. Katagiri Roshi told this story several times in talks that I heard. I found his affect when telling the story authentically light and bemused, quite the opposite of what I imagined myself feeling in such a situation.

"Practice secretly, like a fool, like an idiot," comes from a key source-text for Soto Zen, "The Jeweled Mirror Samadhi," attributed to the Chinese master Dongshan (807–69). This translation is from *Soto School Scriptures for Daily Services and Practice*. Many versions also can be found online. See Andy Ferguson's very useful *Zen's Chinese Heritage: The Masters and their Teachings* for more about Dongshan. For a lot more, see William F. Powell's *The Record of Tung-shan*.

I found the metaphor for Zen training, a country person learning to walk like a city person, in *Dogen's Extensive Record: A Translation of the Eihei Koroku*, translated by Taigen Dan Leighton and Shohaku Okumura, 203. The *Eihei Koroku* is a collection of over 500 of Dogen's talks to his monks and may be even more important for the practice of Soto Zen than his *Shobogenzo*. The translators have made an enormous contribution to Dogen study and practice.

Dogen seems to have had an unusually detailed interest in how to perform excretory bodily functions. See "Washing" *("Senjo")* in Nishijima and Cross' translation *Master Dogen's Shobogenzo, Book 1*, 57–67. This chapter contains the instructions for clay balls as one way of wiping, but only one way. Other Dogen-authorized methods include using old paper and the famous shit stick. Dogen also admonishes against talking or joking with the person in the next stall as well as singing or reciting verses while defecating. He explicitly prohibits graffiti with the shit-stick.

CHAPTER 7: CLEANING UNDER THE HEDGE

Charlotte Joko Beck amplifies a similar point about getting and giving in "The Talk Nobody Wants to Hear," *Nothing Special: Living Zen*, 57–66.

For a classical model of Zen development, see John Daido Loori's *Path of Enlightenment: Stages in a Spiritual Journey*, an unpacking of the Ten Oxherding Pictures.

For an ecumenical and unsurpassed treatment of stages and the spiritual path, see Evelyn Underhill's early-twentieth-century classic, *Mysticism: The Nature and Development of Spiritual Consciousness.*

CHAPTER 8: DOES ZEN HAVE MORALS?

Katagiri Roshi told the bath story many times. See San Francisco Zen Center's *Wind Bell,* Summer 1971, 4, for a similar version. Katagiri Roshi's comments on *nen,* thought moments, also appear in this issue of *Wind Bell.*

The story of Baizhang can be found in Thomas Cleary's *Saying and Doings of Pai-Chang: Ch'an Master of Great Wisdom,* 26. I've changed the pronoun to fit with the bodhisattva Prajnaparamita. A talk titled "Taking Responsibility," by one of the old grandfathers of modern Zen, Aitken Roshi, applies this story to political action. It can be found at www.bpfradio.org/audiopages/0706-AikenRoshi/AitkenRoshi-0706.html.

Sallie Tisdale's thoughts on karma can be found in her important work *Women of the Way: Discovering 2,500 Years of Buddhist Wisdom,* 15.

CHAPTER 9: GAZING AT THE MOON

The version of the "Changsha the Tiger" used here is from *Entangling Vines: Zen Koans of the* Shumon Kattoshu, translated by Thomas Yuho Kirchner, 115.

This chapter shows Katagiri Roshi as a married priest eating meat and drinking alcohol like more than 80% of Japanese Soto Zen priests—surprising, perhaps, given Buddhism's reputation of celibate, vegetarian, non-drinking monks. In rule if not in actual behavior, Buddhist monks throughout Asia do not marry, eat meat, or drink alcohol. Japanese priests and their Western descendents are an anomaly. How did this difference develop? See *Neither Monk nor Layman: Clerical Marriage in Modern Japanese Buddhism* by

Richard Jaffe for an illuminating and careful historical examination of these developments.

CHAPTER 10: BOWING IS LIKE A ROCK IN YOUR HEART

The translation of the key passage from Dogen Zenji's "Negotiating the Way" can be found in Hee-Jin Kim's *Dogen on Meditation and Thinking: A Reflection on His View of Zen*, 21.

The "Genjo-koan" passage is taken from *Flowers of Emptiness: Selections from Dogen's* Shobogenzo, also translated by Hee-Jin Kim, 52.

The story of Huangbo bowing and not seeking Buddha is adapted from Andy Ferguson's translation in *Zen's Chinese Heritage: The Masters and Their Teachings*, 119.

CHAPTER 11: NOT USING ZAZEN

The Dogen passage on "taking up the one thing" comes from *The Wholehearted Way*, 34–35, translated by Taigen Dan Leighton and Shohaku Okumura. "The Wholehearted Way" refers to Dogen's "Bendowa," also translated as "Negotiating the Way" in this volume.

Dale S. Wright's book, *Philosophical Meditations on Zen Buddhism*, is a fascinating study of the effects that our Western worldview have on our understanding of the Dharma. You can find the quoted passage in his "Conclusion: Zen in Theory in Practice," 212.

"Observing," as in "observing the body as not pure," is literally "vipassana" meaning insight, clear seeing, deep seeing, or discernment. This passage and Katagiri Roshi's comment on "Dharani" are from the Minnesota Zen Center's *Udumbara: Journal of Zen Practice*, vol. 4, no. 1 (1987), translated by Katagiri Roshi, Kenneth Port, and Dosho Port, somewhat re-worked by the author.

Dharani are mnemonic devices that through sound express the meaning of Buddha's teaching. Dharani are also believed to function like talismans, protecting the one intoning the dharani or those to whom it is dedicated from disaster and misfortune.

CHAPTER 12: ON BEING DUPED

"The Core of Masculinity" can be found in *The Essential Rumi,* translated by Coleman Barks and John Moyne, 115.

Regarding abuse, see the *Dhammapada: The Sayings of the Buddha,* chapter 1, verse 3, translated by Thomas Cleary: "'He reviled me; he injured me; he defeated me; he deprived.' Those who harbor such grudges, hatred never ceases."

The words of Katagiri Roshi in this chapter can be found in unedited form in the CD "Devotion," December 1988.

This "Genjo-koan" passage is from Kazuaki Tanahashi, *Moon in a Dewdrop: Writings of Zen Master Dogen.*

"Zuigan calls 'Master,'" can be found in Zenkei Shibayama, *Zen Comments on the Mumonkan,* 91.

CHAPTER 13: DAININ'S FOUR ESSENTIAL POINTS

Katagiri Roshi quotes in this chapter can be found in the CD "The Priesthood," December 17, 1980.

Tanahashi's comments on Dogen can be found in his introduction to his beautiful translations of Dogen, *Moon in a Dewdrop: Writings of Zen Master Dogen,* edited by Kazuaki Tanahashi, 22.

Kim's comments on Dogen and his careful consideration of practice-enlightenment can be found in *Dogen on Meditation and Thinking: A Reflection on His View of Zen,* 22. The quote from "Negotiating the Way" is Hee-Jin Kim's translation.

The poem by Dragon Fang was translated by Katagiri Roshi and given to his priests.

CHAPTER 14: THROWING OPEN THE HEART

This story comes from a CD by Katagiri Roshi, "Mindfulness," March 23, 1984.

Chögyam Trungpa Rinpoche's thoughts on Zen can be found in "Zen Mind Vajra Mind," *Buddhadharma,* Fall 2007: 43.

Katagiri Roshi's comments on "spirit" and direct, immediate actualizing of it are from "The Priesthood," December 17, 1980, CD.

CHAPTER 15: MAYBE NEXT LIFE

Robert Thurman's comments on the little seed that fuels our sense of disconnection is from "Reincarnation: A Debate," *Tricycle: The Buddhist Review,* Summer 1997, between Robert Thurman and Stephen Batchelor. The debate vividly presents two sides of the karma and rebirth issue—the more traditionalist view of Thurman and the interpretationalist view of Batchelor.

For more on the important issue of karma in the contemporary world, see Dale S. Wright's "Critical Questions Toward a Naturalized Concept of Karma in Buddhism," *The Journal of Buddhist Ethics,* vol. 11, 2004. This online journal has many other well-thought through essays as well.

For an easy-to-read summary of Michel Foucault's work on power see David White's "Responding to Personal Failure," *The International Journal of Narrative Therapy and Community Work,* no. 3, 2002.

"Conjecturing about an unconjecturable" can be found online in Thanissaro Bhikkhu's translation of the "Acintita Sutta: Unconjecturable," at www.accesstoinsight.org/tipitaka/an/an04/an04.077.than.html. I've adjusted the wording slightly to fit with the context here.

The passages on the Wild Fox koan are from Dogen's "Great

Practice" *("Daishugyo")* from an unpublished translation by Kazaki Tanahashi and Dojun Dan Welch.

For the metaphor about parfait, I'm indebted to Donkey in the movie, *Shrek.*

The quote from the *Lotus Sutra* is from my favorite translation, by Bunno Kato, et al., *The Threefold Lotus Sutra,* 52.

The Bible quote from the "Book of Job" is from the Bible that I was given by the St. Casimir's Guild in Cloquet, Minnesota, when I graduated from high school in 1974—*The New American Bible,* 599.

The poem excerpt by W.S. Merwin is from "Fox Sleep" in *The Vixen.* This collection of poems weaves references to the Wild Fox koan together with the deep emotions surrounding love, place, and death.

CHAPTER 16: HAIR ON FIRE

I'm indebted to Jan Freier, a longtime Zen student, delightful story-teller, and fine human being for the anecdote that begins this chapter.

The lyrics of Bob Dylan are from "Mississippi," on the CD *Love and Theft.*

Dogen's imagined response to Shakespeare is lifted from "Guidelines for Studying the Way," translated by Kazuaki Tana-hashi and Ed Brown, *Moon in a Dewdrop: Writings of Zen Master Dogen,* 31.

Henry David Thoreau's words on men snoring are from the "Conclusion" to *Walden.*

Ikkyu's powerful poetry is from Stephen Berg's luminous trans-lation, *Crow with No Mouth: Ikkyu 15th Century Zen Master.*

Bibliography

Aitken, Robert. 1994. *The Practice of Perfection: The Paramitas from a Zen Buddhist Perspective.* Washington, D.C.: Counterpoint.

————. Robert. 2006. "Taking Responsibility." BPFRadio.org: A Production of the Buddhist Peace Fellowship. Available at http://www.bpfradio.org (accessed March 30, 2008).

Barks, Coleman and John Moyne, trans. 1995. *The Essential Rumi.* New York: HarperCollins Publishers.

Beck, Charlotte Joko. 1993. *Nothing Special: Living Zen.* New York: HarperCollins Publishers.

Berg, Stephen. 1989. *Crow With No Mouth: Ikkyu 15th Century Zen Master.* Port Townsend: Copper Canyon Press.

Bodhi, Bhikku, trans. 2000. *The Connected Discourses of the Buddha: A New Translation of the Samyutta Nikaya.* Boston: Wisdom Publications.

Catholic Book Association of America. 1970. *The New American Bible.* New York: Catholic Book Publishing Co.

Cleary, Thomas, trans. 1978. *Saying and Doings of Pai-Chang: Ch'an Master of Great Wisdom.* Los Angeles: Center Publications.

_____, trans. 1995. *Dhammapada: The Sayings of the Buddha.* New York: Bantam Books.

Ferguson, Andrew. 2000. *Zen's Chinese Heritage: The Masters and Their Teachings.* Boston: Wisdom Publications.

Heine, Steven. 1994. *Dogen and the Koan Tradition: A Tale of Two Shobogenzo Texts.* Albany: State University of New York Press.

_____. "Abbreviation or Aberration: The Role of Shushogi in Modern Soto Zen Buddhism." In *Buddhism in the Modern World: Adaptations of an Ancient Tradition.* Edited by Steven Heine and Charles S. Prebish. Oxford: 2003: Oxford University Press.

_____. 2008. *Zen Skin, Zen Marrow: Will the Real Zen Buddhism Please Stand Up?* New York: Oxford University Press.

Heine, Steven and Dale S. Wright (editors). 2000. *The Koan: Texts and Contexts in Zen Buddhism.* New York: Oxford University Press.

Jaffe, Richard M. 2001. *Neither Monk nor Layman: Clerical Marriage in Modern Japanese Buddhism.* Princeton: Princeton University Press.

Katagiri, Dainin. "The Four Vows." *Wind Bell,* vol. X, no. 1, Summer 1971.

_____. "The Priesthood," December 17, 1980. CD. Minneapolis: Minnesota Zen Meditation Center.

_____. "Digesting Zazen Koan," March 12, 1983. CD. Minneapolis: Minnesota Zen Meditation Center.

_____. "Mindfulness," March 23, 1984. CD. Minneapolis: Minnesota Zen Meditation Center.

Katagiri, Dainin with Kenneth Port and Dosho Port. "Mindfulness." *Udumbara: Journal of Zen Practice,* vol. 4, no. 1, 1987.

Katagiri, Dainin. "Review and Renew Buddhism for the Twenty-first Century," October 5, 1988. CD. Minneapolis: Minnesota Zen Meditation Center.

_____. "Devotion: Walking Alone with Open Heart," December 24, 1988. CD. Minneapolis: Minnesota Zen Meditation Center.

_____. 1988. *Returning to Silence: Zen Practice in Daily Life.* Boston and London: Shambhala Publications.

Kato, Bunno, and Yoshiro Tamura. 1975. *The Threefold Lotus Sutra.* New York: Weatherhill.

Kim, Hee-Jin, trans. 1985. *Flowers of Emptiness: Selections from Dogen's* Shobogenzo. Lewiston, New York: The Edwin Mellen Press.

_____. 2007. *Dogen on Meditation and Thinking: A Reflection on His View of Zen.* Albany: State University Press.

Kirchner, Thomas Yuho. 2004. *Entangling Vines: Zen Koans of the Shumon Kattoshu.* Kyoto: Tenruy-ji Institute for Philosophy and Religion.

Leighton, Taigen Dan and Shohaku Okumura, trans. 1997. *The Wholehearted Way: A Translation of Eihei Dogen's* Bendowa.

Leighton, Taigen Dan and Shohaku Okumura, trans. 2004. *Dogen's Extensive Record: A Translation of the Eihei Koroku.* Boston: Wisdom Publications.

Loori, John Daido. 1999. *Path of Enlightenment: Stages in a Spiritual Journey.* Mt. Tremper, New York: Dharma Communications Press.

Loori, John Daido. 2002. *The Art of Just Sitting: Essential Writings on the Zen Practice of Shikantaza.* Boston: Wisdom Publications.

Loori, John Daido and Tom Kirchner. 2005. *Sitting with Koans: Essential Writings on the Zen Practice of Koan Study.* Boston: Wisdom Publications.

Loori, John Daido and Kazuaki Tanahashi. 2005. *The True Dharma Eye: Zen Master Dogen's Three Hundred Koans.* Boston: Shambhala Publications.

Merwin, W.S. 2002. *The Vixen.* New York: Alfred A. Knopf.

Nishijima, Gudo and Chodo Cross. 1999. *Master Dogen's Shobo-genzo: Books 1–4*. London: Windbell Publications.

Ogui, Socho Koshin. Interview by Clark Strand. "Ordinary Struggles." *Tricycle: The Buddhist Review* (Summer 2006).

Powell, William F., trans. 1986. *The Record of Tung-shan*. Honolulu: University of Hawaii Press.

Sasaki, Ruth Fuller, Yoshitaka Iriya, and Dana Fraser. 1971. *A Man of Zen: The Recorded Sayings of Layman P'ang*. New York and London: Weatherhill.

Senzaki, Nyogen and Ruth Strout McCandless. 1961. *The Iron Flute: 100 Zen Koans*. Rutland, Vermont: Charles E. Tuttle Company.

Shibayama, Zenkei. 1974. *Zen Comments on the Mumonkan*. San Francisco: Harper & Row.

Sotoshu Sumucho. 2001. *Soto School Scriptures for Daily Services and Practice*. Tokyo: Sotoshu Sumucho.

Tanahashi, Kazuaki. 1985. *Moon in a Dewdrop: Writings of Zen Master Dogen*. New York: North Point Press.

Tarrant, John. 2008. *Bring Me the Rhinoceros and Other Zen Koans to Bring You Joy*. New York: Harmony Books.

Thanissaro, Bhikku, trans. "Acintita Sutta: Unconjecturable." *Access to Insight*. Available at http://www.accesstoinsight.org/tipitaka/an/an04/an04.077.than.html (accessed November 20, 2007).

Thoreau, Henry David. 1958. *Walden and Civil Disobedience.* New York: Harper & Row.

Thurman, Robert. "Reincarnation: A Debate." *Tricycle: The Buddhist Review,* Summer 1997.

Tisdale, Sallie. 2005. *Women of the Way: Discovering 2,500 Years of Buddhist Wisdom.* New York: HarperCollins.

Trungpa, Chögyam. "Zen Mind, Vajra Mind." *Buddhadhama: The Practitioner's Quarterly,* Fall 2007.

Underhill, Evelyn. 1993. *Mysticism: The Nature and Development of Spiritual Consciousness.* Oxford: Oneworld Publications.

White, David. "Responding to Personal Failure." In *The International Journal of Narrative Therapy and Community Work,* no. 3, 2002.

Wright, Dale S. "Critical Questions Toward a Naturalized Concept of Karma in Buddhism." *The Journal of Buddhist Ethics,* vol. 11, 2004. Available at www.buddhistethics.org (accessed September 15, 2007).

Wright, Dale S. 1998. *Philosophical Meditations on Zen Buddhism.* New York: Cambridge University Press.

About the Author

D OSHO PORT is a Zen priest and Dharma heir of Dainin Katagiri in the Soto Zen tradition. He has also trained with Tangen Harada, Thich Nhat Hanh, and John Daido Loori. Dosho teaches with Wild Fox Zen at Transforming Through Play Temple in White Bear, Minnesota. He is a half-time single parent of two wonderful children and the program lead in a school for adolescents with severe behavior problems. Dosho can be found in the blog world at wildfoxzen.blogspot.com. He lives in White Bear Township, Minnesota.

About Wisdom Publications

WISDOM PUBLICATIONS, a nonprofit publisher, is dedicated to making available authentic works relating to Buddhism for the benefit of all. We publish books by ancient and modern masters in all traditions of Buddhism, translations of important texts, and original scholarship. Additionally, we offer books that explore East-West themes unfolding as traditional Buddhism encounters our modern culture in all its aspects. Our titles are published with the appreciation of Buddhism as a living philosophy, and with the special commitment to preserve and transmit important works from Buddhism's many traditions.

To learn more about Wisdom, or to browse books online, visit our website at www.wisdompubs.org.

You may request a copy of our catalog online or by writing to this address:

Wisdom Publications
199 Elm Street
Somerville, Massachusetts 02144 USA

Telephone: 617-776-7416
Fax: 617-776-7841
Email: info@wisdompubs.org
www.wisdompubs.org

THE WISDOM TRUST

As a nonprofit publisher, Wisdom is dedicated to the publication of Dharma books for the benefit of all sentient beings and dependent upon the kindness and generosity of sponsors in order to do so. If you would like to make a donation to Wisdom, you may do so through our website or our Somerville office. If you would like to help sponsor the publication of a book, please write or email us at the address above.

Thank you.

Wisdom is a nonprofit, charitable 501(c)(3) organization affiliated with the Foundation for the Preservation of the Mahayana Tradition (FPMT).

WISDOM PUBLICATIONS

199 Elm Street · Somerville MA 02144 USA

Please return this card if you would like to be kept informed about our current and future publications.

Name _____

Street _____

City _____ State/Prov. _____

Country _____ Zip _____

                                                    New Address? ❑

_____ Email _____

In which book did you find this card? _____

How did you find out about this book? _____

Where did you buy this book? _____

Do you subscribe to any of the following magazines?

❑ Tricycle   ❑ Shambhala Sun   ❑ Inquiring Mind   ❑ Yoga Journal   ❑ Parabola

❑ Buddhadharma ❑ Mother Jones ❑ Yoga International ❑ Mountain Record ❑ The Dot

❑ other: _____

visit us at

www.wisdompubs.org for book excerpts and special offers

Wisdom Publications is a nonprofit charitable organization.